True New Engla[nd]

Mysteries • Ghosts
Crimes • Oddities

Charles Turek Robinson

Illustrations by B. Turek Robinson

Published by Covered Bridge Press
7 Adamsdale Road
North Attleborough, Massachusetts 02760

Library of Congress Cataloging-in-Publication Data

Robinson, Charles Turek, 1962-
  True New England mysteries, ghosts, crimes,
  oddities / Charles Turek Robinson
      p.   cm.
  Includes bibliographical references.
  ISBN 0-924771-97-6 (paper)
  1. New England—History—Anecdotes. 2. New
England—Social life and customs—Anecdotes.
3. Curiosities and wonders—New England—Anecdotes.
I. Title.
F4.6.R63   1997
001.94'0974—DC21

DEDICATION

As always, to my loving parents

ACKNOWLEDGEMENTS

The author wishes to thank the following societies and publications for their valuable assistance:

University of Vermont College of Medicine
The Lynn Historical Society
The Fall River Historical Society
Douglas Charles Press
The Providence Journal-Bulletin
The Rehoboth Reporter
John Jay Library at Brown University
Yankee Magazine

Special thanks to my publisher, Chuck Durang
of Covered Bridge Press

Critical Acclaim for Mr. Robinson's
Previous Books on New England History and Lore

"When it comes to generating goosebumps, none hold a candle to (Charles Robinson)."
— *Yankee*

"Mr. Robinson takes (history and lore) a step further than other reporters."
— *The Boston Herald*

"(His work) echoes with ghoulish laughter...Here comes Charles Robinson...to disturb your peace."
— *The Providence Journal*

"Robinson's work is excellent...The author has done a good job of researching and presenting his material."
— *WVPR Public Radio Vermont*

Table of Contents

Three: Amazing Yankees

Four: New England Enigmas

INTRODUCTION

Welcome to the New England netherworld – a darker, shadowy realm of New England history in which dwell the 17th, 18th, and 19th-century perpetrators of the region's most horrific and bloody crimes (including unlikely fiends of often high social standing, such as Lizzie Borden and the homicidal minister Ephraim Avery – two of many such historical New England criminals discussed in this book, often in a new light based on the latest, most up-to-date, non-sensational research).

Compiled by best-selling New England author Charles Robinson with careful research methods deriving from his anthropological graduate training, this book guides the reader into other unsettling areas of New England's shadowy netherworld – from unsolved, inexplicable New England mysteries to carefully documented "haunted" New England homes and graveyards to...well, all sorts of unexplained New England occurrences that have been thoughtfully researched and carefully selected for this book.

Of course, as for the ghost accounts, there is no way to empirically "prove" that some of these very odd New England occurrences actually took place. However, the reader can rest assured that the author has carefully screened all alleged accounts and witnesses for sincerity, consistency, appropriate effect and depth of emotion. The reports contained in this book are like no others in print, and the author's previously published ghost research has been called the most believable in its genre by publications like *Yankee* and *The Boston Herald*.

True New England Mysteries, Ghosts, Crimes & Oddities

This unusual book also explores other New England oddities; most notably, eccentric, astounding New England characters who were far ahead of their times and who attained truly astonishing feats. For instance, there was Annie Smith Peck, who, in her sixties and even into her eighties, broke mountain-climbing records around the world at the turn-of-the-century. And then there was Dallas Boushey, who worked his way up to become the University of Vermont School of Medicine's most respected professor of anatomy...even though he was an eighth-grade drop-out! And, of course, we cannot forget Deborah Sampson Gannet, who fought bravely in the American Revolution – successfully disguised as a man!

The above facts are just a small sampling of the startling, true-life New England "weirdness" – historical and otherwise – that you'll encounter in this fascinating, unprecedented book – a thoughtfully researched study compiled by a historical researcher whose work has been critically acclaimed by some of New England's most important and prestigious publications.

Frank DeMattos

President, Anawan Historical Society

CHAPTER ONE

NOTORIOUS NEW ENGLANDERS

A GALLERY OF ROGUES

New England history, like human nature itself, has a dark side. The towns of early New England were not as picture-perfectly wholesome as we might like to think. Historical analysis is, first and foremost, a study of people, including some people we might like to forget. But we cannot distill history, lest it become, well, boring. That said, let us take a step back into the past, where we will meet some ladies and gentlemen who were anything but ladies and gentlemen. All of the following characters are historically factual. They all lived in New England:

JOHN BILLINGTON (d. 1630): Mr. John Billington, who resided in Plymouth, Massachusetts, has the dubious honor of being America's first murderer. Billington was a coarse, rowdy Londoner who came to Plymouth on the Mayflower in 1620. He was no perfect Pilgrim, and he was especially fond of swearing at his religiously pious fellows, who often responded by throwing him into the stocks. And each time John was released from the stocks, what do you think he immediately said to those who had put him there? "*#*&#*!" and "#!*#&*!" were his favorites. Back to the stocks once again.

John Billington became the black sheep of Plymouth Colony. When he was not swearing at his Pilgrim brethren, he was punching them out. He loved to fight. John developed a particularly nasty loathing toward fellow settler John Newcomen. The basis of the feud is unclear, though its ugly outcome is known only too well. One day in 1630, Billington hid himself behind a rock. When John Newcomen strolled by, Billington rudely greeted him with a fatal blast from his blunderbuss. Swearing is one thing, but murder tended to be particularly unpopular among the pious Pilgrims. John Billington, America's first historically documented murderer, was promptly hanged.

BATHSHEBA SPOONER (d. 1778): Born in 1746, Bathsheba was the daughter of a wealthy Massachusetts landholder. In 1766, she married a squire named Joshua Spooner, and the couple resided on a comfortable estate in Brookfield, Massachusetts. It seems unlikely that Bathsheba loved her husband very much, especially considering that she had him murdered.

It all began at the end of the Revolutionary War. Ezra Ross, a young soldier passing through Brookfield on his way home from battle, stopped by the Spooner estate and asked for a meal. Joshua was away, and Bathsheba's generosity poured forth. The attractive housewife not only fed the hungry soldier, but she also invited him into her bed. A torrid affair ensued, and Bathsheba immediately began to worry about her husband. What if he found out? Being a practical woman, Bathsheba soon reasoned that the affair would not bother her husband if he were, well, dead.

The housewife asked her new lover to kill him. Ezra, grateful that his meal had come with such a pleasant dessert, agreed. He enlisted the help of two fellow soldiers, and the three men killed Joshua as he stepped onto the porch of his Brookfield home. They hid the body in a nearby well and were soon

3

arrested sporting about in the victim's clothes. Bathsheba was implicated, and a Massachusetts court sentenced her and the others to death. The housewife protested that she was pregnant, but a court-appointed midwife testified otherwise. Bathsheba was hanged in Worcester, Massachusetts, on July 2, 1778, and hers was the first criminal execution in post-Revolutionary Massachusetts. A postmortem revealed that she was, in fact, five months with child.

WILLIAM BEADLE (d. 1783): Mrs. Beadle, a Connecticut housewife, should have known that something was wrong with her husband. Something, indeed, was bothering William, for he had developed the ominous habit of taking a tremendous ax and butcher knife to bed with him. He also stopped talking completely. But Mrs. Beadle was the unquestioning sort. If her husband wanted to sleep with a large ax and butcher knife at his side, that was his right.

Mrs. Beadle should have realized that most people who take large cutting instruments to bed with them are probably not normal. On the morning of December 11, 1783, Mrs. Beadle got a crash course in abnormal human psychology: William's ax came crashing down on her head. William then committed suicide, saving Connecticut authorities the trouble of hanging him.

ABRAHAM PRESCOTT (d. 1836): Some people have learned to handle rejection gracefully. Others have not. On June 23, 1833, in Pembroke, New Hampshire, Sally Cochran refused to make love to seventeen-year-old Abraham Prescott. Abraham's feelings were hurt. And when people hurt Abraham's feelings, he had a nasty habit of wanting to kill them.

In this instance, he did just that. When arrested for having fatally hit Sally over the head with a stake, Abraham confessed to the crime. His defense, however, was no ordinary one: the boy claimed that he had been asleep when he committed the act! Abraham was a chronic sleepwalker, argued his lawyers, and he had not been awake at the time of the murder. They suggested that he was therefore not responsible for the crime.

The jury, for some strange reason, didn't buy it. Abraham was hanged, wide awake, in Hopkinton, New Hampshire, in 1836.

THOMAS THATCHER GRAVES (d. 1898): Our last "rogue" in this section is Dr. Graves, whose killing of Josephine Barnaby in 1893 became one of America's classic murders. Josephine was the wife of a Providence, Rhode Island, clothing merchant. When her wealthy husband died, she found herself cut out of his estate, apparently due to their marital discord. Thomas T. Graves, who was the woman's physician, pitied her predicament, so much so that he helped her contest her husband's will. Thanks to the doctor's kind efforts, the widow's inheritance was restored.

But Dr. Graves' efforts were not *that* kind. As soon as Josephine received her part of the estate, Graves commenced to steal it from her. As the woman's physician, he insisted that she travel for "health reasons." While she was away, he systematically robbed her of her assets. Eventually, the widow caught on. She wrote to Dr. Graves from Denver, threatening to expose him.

5

The sinister doctor would have none of that. So, he poisoned a bottle of whiskey and anonymously sent it to Josephine. The tainted bottle was accompanied by a note: "To Josephine-Please accept this fine old whiskey from your friend in the woods." The woman and a friend sampled the mysterious sender's "fine" whiskey. For both of them, that drink was their last one.

Suspicion for the murder immediately fell on the Rhode Island physician. In court, Graves strongly claimed his innocence; that is, until one Joseph Breslyn showed up. Breslyn testified that, some months earlier, the doctor had approached him in a Boston train station, claiming that he could not write and asking the stranger if he would be so kind as to pen a note for him. Breslyn had agreed, and Dr. Graves had dictated as follows: "To Josephine-Please accept this fine old whiskey from your friend in the woods." The physician, it seems, had not wanted his own handwriting to be traced. Breslyn's testimony convicted Graves. In April, 1893, Dr. Graves beat the hangman to his task. He fatally overdosed himself with poison in his prison cell.

ORGANIZED CRIME
ALIVE AND WELL IN COLONIAL NEW ENGLAND

Lest we should think that the sleepy country villages of yesteryear were models of wholesome quaintness, let us consider the case of Mary (Peck) Butterworth, the wily mastermind of Rehoboth, Massachusetts' first (and only) professional counterfeiting ring. In August of 1724, a warrant issued by a Rhode Island court called for the arrest of Mary and "other Sundry persons, inhabitants of Rehoboth...(who) in said county are vehemently Suspected to be Guilty of Making Counterfeiting and Uttering the bills of Publick Credit." Exposed by a former associate, Mary and her counterfeiting cohorts were arrested in Rehoboth and taken to Bristol, Rhode Island, for arraignment. Despite an abundance of incriminating testimony against the defendants, the court eventually acquitted the lot of them, though to this day an even cursory review of the case suggests that Mary and her bunch were, indeed, up to their elbows in wet ink.

Who was Mary (Peck) Butterworth, and how did she become, in the words of Rehoboth historian Richard Bowen, the most "successful... and biggest single (colonial) counterfeiter in New England?" Unfortunately, we know little of Mary's early life, though town records tell us she was born in 1686 to Elizabeth and Joseph Peck, the proprietors of a small Rehoboth tavern. In 1711, at age twenty-five, Elizabeth married John Butterworth, Jr., a fairly well-off housewright. The young couple resided in Rehoboth, and within a few years Mary was tending to several small children. It seems, however, that

Mary's was an ambitious soul. Despite her husband's good income, and despite the obligations of motherhood (Mary, in fact, seems to have been an attentive mother), the young housewife saw fit to pursue her own profession. The profession she chose was anything but dainty.

By the early 1700's, counterfeiting of state-issued paper currency was rampant in New England. Most counterfeiters, however, were mere bunglers of their trade, and their poorly engraved copper plates usually landed them in the stocks. It took the cunning of an obscure Rehoboth housewife to transform the crude craft into a criminal art form of masterful precision. In 1716, Mary set up shop in her kitchen, where she cooked up what were probably the most artfully deceptive counterfeit bills of her day. Years later, a witness who had observed Mary's operation described her method as follows:

She Layed a Piece of fine water starched musoline upon them (the genuine bills) and so Plucked out the Letters upon Said musoline & then Layed the musoline upon a clean Piece of Paper and so made ye impression of the Letters (on the blank paper). She afterward went over the Letters with a fine pen. (From the deposition of Nicholas Camp of Rehoboth, taken at Newport—August, 1723)

The procedure also entailed carefully heating the water-starched muslin so that it would effectively lift the impression of the genuine bill and transfer it to the blank paper. In its simplicity, Mary's method was ingenious. It allowed her to operate without any of the incriminating equipment (metal plates, printing tools, etc.) which, if discovered, would mean certain criminal conviction. When finished with the muslin, Mary had simply to toss it into the fireplace, and all traces of her dubious doings were gone.

Shrewd in counterfeiting, and even more shrewd in business, Mary established a network of agents to distribute her bogus wares. Several of these accomplices were distinguished Rehoboth citizens and included the town's Deputy Sheriff, Daniel Smith. Clearly, a Rehoboth scandal was in the making. As her operation expanded, Mary also hired her three brothers, Israel, Stephen, and Nicholas, along with Nicholas' wife, Hannah, to assist her in her kitchen print shop. Before long, Mary was able to extend her "product line" to include bills from Massachusetts, Rhode Island, and Connecticut. There is evidence that Mary's

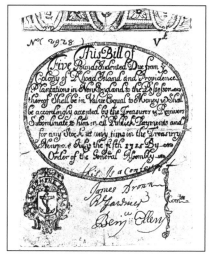

One of Mary's masterfully-wrought counterfeit bills.

husband, John Butterworth, Jr., gleefully supported the thriving enterprise. John, perhaps, considered himself lucky. At a time when most husbands had to give their wives money, John had a wife who simply printed her own!

For seven lucrative years, from 1716-1723, the money shop of Mary (Peck) Butterworth was open for business. Through her well-organized distribution network, Mary marketed her bills for approximately half face value (i.e. each five pound note sold for two and a half pounds in genuine currency). There was, apparently, no shortage of takers, and estimates suggest that Mary manufactured considerably more than a thousand pounds, certainly a significant amount in those days. Clearly, organized crime was alive and well in colonial Rehoboth.

But it would not last. There was one flaw in Mary's otherwise exquisite criminal career. Quite simply, she became perilously overconfident in her ability to evade detection, and she became less discreet in her selection of associates. In describing her step-by-step counterfeiting method to Nicholas Camp of Rehoboth, Mary made a dire mistake. In 1723, after being apprehended by authorities for suspicion of counterfeiting, Camp divulged the full nature and extent of Mary's illicit activities. Mary was promptly arrested, along with her husband, brothers, and sister-in-law.

In the end, however, the cunning Mary (Peck) Butterworth would prevail. Despite Camp's incriminating and seemingly reliable testimony, Mary and her associates were acquitted for "lack of evidence." This pardon is perhaps not surprising when we consider that Mary was the daughter of one of the most important and influential pioneer families in Rehoboth...all of the town and colony officers were her relatives. In addition, Mary had been clever enough to operate without incriminating metal plates and printing equipment. Mary was soon freed, though her arrest apparently did shake some sense into her. She never resumed her illicit activities, and she died in 1775, at the age of 89, without having ever paid for her notorious crime.

THE MURDEROUS MINISTER

Sixty years before Lizzie Borden wielded her ax, another murder was in the forefront of the American consciousness. Until Lizzie stole the spotlight, the Reverend Ephraim Kingsbury Avery held the dubious distinction of being Southeastern New England's (and the nation's) most notorious murder suspect.

Sarah Cornell, 30 and unmarried, was a weaver in a Fall River, Massachusetts, factory. She was also pregnant. And when, on December 21, 1832, a farmer found her body hanging from a haystack on the outskirts of town, not too far from Rehoboth, he thought he had stumbled upon a suicide.

A coroner's inquest determined otherwise. The young woman's body was badly bruised, her hair and clothing disheveled. She had probably been beaten and strangled, then hung to mimic a

The Durfee Farm, where Sarah's body was found, as it actually appeared in 1832. Artist's copy of a 19th-century engraving

suicide. The victim had few friends and no nearby relatives. But she did have close ties to Ephraim Kingsbury Avery, a married and respected Methodist minister from Bristol, Rhode Island.

Sarah's physician soon came forward with some startling news. The young woman had named Reverend Avery as the father of her unborn child. When authorities searched Sarah's Fall River boarding house, they found an incriminating letter – a letter in which the handwriting bore a peculiar resemblance to Reverend Avery's.

The author of the correspondence had requested a meeting with the woman, specifying a particular day and place – the same day and place of Sarah's murder. The letter was unsigned, but according to the courier who had delivered it to Sarah, it had been posted by the minister. There was also a curious unpunctuated note that had been written by the victim herself, apparently just before leaving her residence on the day of the incident: *"If I should be missing inquire of the Rev Mr Avery of Bristol he will know where I am Dec 20 S M Cornell."*

Inquire they did. Reverend Avery, proclaiming his innocence but unable to prove his whereabouts at the time of the murder, was promptly arrested. A preliminary hearing was held in Bristol. While prosecuting attorneys were able to establish both motive and opportunity, they could offer no witnesses to the crime nor anything beyond circumstantial evidence. Avery was discharged by the court. However, public agitation in Fall River soon resulted in new charges against the minister.

The mobs cried for blood, and the case drew national attention. In the meantime, Reverend Avery fled to New Hampshire. Officials eventually caught up with the fugitive and returned him for trial, which was held before a special session of the Rhode Island Supreme Court during May and June of 1833.

The trial was socially explosive. Vying for acquittal were the Methodists, who were already suspect in a New England dominated by Calvinism. The conviction of one of their ministers could bring further scorn to the church. It was up to their attorneys to prove that Sarah had been promiscuous, that any of a number of men could have fathered the baby, and that the death had actually been a suicide.

Pushing for conviction were the powerful Fall River industrialists. Their public relations position had always been that factory work away from home did not hinder the moral development of a young woman. Avery's conviction would show that Sarah's pregnancy had not resulted from promiscuity fostered by her factory life outside the household, but was due to her wicked seduction by a trusted clergyman.

Both the Methodists and the industrialists undoubtedly had a hand in orchestrating the testimony of witnesses, who contradicted each other on a number of points. But, by the end of the trial, the prosecution had the advantage. Medical testimony showed that murder was much more plausible than suicide. Avery had no good alibi, and, in addition to testimony which clearly linked him to the letter that had set up the fateful meeting, a number of people testified that an unfamiliar man closely resembling Avery had entered Fall River on the day of the crime.

13

Yet, the jury responded by finding the minister not guilty, a verdict that was no doubt influenced by a defense strategy which included viciously assailing the victim's moral character. To a greater extent than the minister, Sarah herself had been posthumously placed on trial. It was a case in which Avery's attorneys had originated, or at the very least perfected, a questionable defense tactic that persists to this day in sexual assault cases: that of attempting to use a female victim's sexual history to shed doubt on the culpability of her assailant.

The public was outraged by the verdict. The minister was hung and burned in effigy in several towns and was tried in the press for some time afterward. In a Boston street, several hundred people mobbed him. A Methodist shopkeeper saved him at the last minute, pulling him into his store and locking out the crowd. The Methodist church did its best to clear the minister's name but failed. Reverend Avery eventually moved with his family to Lorain County, Ohio, where he lived out his life as a failed minister and moderately successful farmer.

WHY DID LIZZIE BORDEN REALLY DO IT?

Of all local mysteries, the case of Lizzie Borden is perhaps the most unsettling and provocative. While most modern historians agree that Lizzie did, in fact, hideously murder her parents with an ax, there is still much disagreement as to why she committed the crime.

Assuming that Lizzie did murder her parents on that horrific August day in 1892 (both circumstantial and trial evidence clearly suggest that she did), we must ask ourselves what would motivate a genteel, upper-class young woman to perpetrate such a fiendish act of violence? The most commonly suggested motive is murder for money (Andrew Borden was one of the richest men in Fall River, and Lizzie stood to gain a lot by his death).

However, in this writer's opinion, the primal and violent nature of the murders suggests a motive that far transcended mere monetary greed. In fact, the murders were so utterly violent and primordial (consisting of forceful, frenetic, repeated ax blows to the heads of the victims) that they attest to a frightening, primal rage on the part of the murderer. The question arises, then: what was the cause of Lizzie's uncontrollable—and ultimately deadly—state of anger?

In attempting to answer this question, it is useful to review what we know about the character and psychological make-up of Lizzie Borden. During her trial, even Lizzie's supporters acknowledged that she was socially withdrawn and maladjusted. Her friends described her as "very sensitive, inclined to be non-communicative with new acquaintances." An otherwise favorable *Boston Herald* article noted that Lizzie "thought people were not favorably disposed toward her and that she made a poor impression." Although she was the daughter of the wealthiest man in town, she never married. In fact, observers noted that Lizzie was inclined to avoid the company of men.

In addition to being pathologically shy and insecure, especially around men, Lizzie had additional problems. Her uncle described her as a "peculiar girl, often given to fits of sullenness." Even more disturbingly, Lizzie was also a kleptomaniac. Long after the murders, at a time when her substantial wealth would have allowed her to buy anything, Lizzie was caught stealing porcelain plates from Tilden-Thurber in Providence. Even before the murders, as a wealthy young girl, Lizzie was known to be a notorious shoplifter in Fall River. Incidents of Lizzie's stealing were reported by such stores as Gifford's Jewelry and Cherry & Web, among others.

Finally, in attempting to fully understand Lizzie's apparent mental instability, we must look at her awkward home life. The Borden home was known to be a place of mistrust, anxiety, and secrecy. Lizzie and her sister continually argued with their father and step-mother. So frequent were the battles that Lizzie and her sister often took their meals at separate times from the elder Bordens. The Borden house itself was a morbid place that tightly locked out the outer world. The outside door had triple locks, and all of the interior doors were also curiously fitted with multiple locks. As a family, the Bordens were strangely secretive, apprehensive, and withdrawn.

Lizzie's quirky personality traits and problems with shoplifting, as well as the secretive, anxious nature of the home in which she lived, may point to a disturbing possibility. In fact, in a recent article, Brown University psychiatrist M. Eileen McNamara suggests that Lizzie's pathological shyness and insecurity around men, as well as the secretive and tense nature of the Borden household, may indicate that Lizzie was the victim of incest. If, in fact, this suspicion is true, it might explain the uncontrollable rage with which Lizzie finally hacked her parents to death. Greed for money would not satisfactorily explain the unrestrained violence by which the murders were characterized. Incest, however, and the frenetic rage it might have produced in its victim, just might explain why the Bordens were killed with such ferocious violence and malevolence.

What evidence is there that Lizzie was sexually abused by her father? Well, as Dr. McNamara notes in her article, "incest survivors carry with them a mix of rage, guilt, and love toward their parents, and feelings of self-loathing. Relationships with others are molded on relationships learned in the home, and incest survivors often have a very difficult time relating to others." Clearly, Lizzie had difficulty relating to others. Additionally, as Dr. McNamara points out, "incest survivors come to feel that their value is in their sexual attractiveness (and Lizzie was known to be a lover of fine clothes—i.e. very concerned about her appearance). Their relationships with other men, also molded after their relationship with their father, are troubled, and some avoid these relationships entirely, preferring the company of women (this description fits Lizzie exactly).

Additionally, according to many psychiatrists, kleptomania and other petty crimes are commonly observed in incest survivors. "The survivors have themselves been robbed," says Dr. McNamara. "Crimes have been done in secret to them, and stealing may recreate these emotions in an attempt at mastery. Like Lizzie, such kleptomaniacs do not steal for want or need. The point of the theft is not gain, but 'getting away' with something forbidden, without detection, like incest." Certainly, "need" played no role whatsoever in Lizzie's strong penchant for theft. Was her inexplicable stealing, then, actually a playing out of some incest-related psycho-drama—one involving "getting away with the forbidden" and trying to "regain mastery," as Dr. McNamara suggests? Clearly, considering that it continued well into her adulthood, Lizzie's fondness for stealing (even though her wealth made it totally unnecessary) remains one of the most puzzling aspects of her personality.

Certain other facts about the case might fit a hypothesis of incest. Lizzie's sister Emma, like Lizzie herself, never married. Around men, she was "shy and retiring," just like her sister. In other words, Emma, too, displayed behavior consistent with that commonly observed in victims of incest. Why did both daughters have problems relating to men? Why did neither ever marry? And why were both Lizzie and Emma, as everyone around them readily noticed, so powerfully jealous of their stepmother? Did they perhaps feel that they were in sexual competition with her—that they had to compete with her for their father's affections?

Why was the Borden household such a secretive place, with an unusual number of locks on the doors? And, as Dr. McNamara notes, "Andrew Borden remarried at age 43. He was wealthy, and one of the richest men in town. Why did he not marry a young attractive woman to gratify his sexual needs? Why did he instead marry a 38-year-old dowdy woman, unattractive and possibly near menopause in those more difficult times? Perhaps his sexual needs were gratified elsewhere."

Perhaps the most convincing bit of evidence is to be found in the violent nature of the murders. Dr. McNamara observes: "If Lizzie killed for money, one might expect that in later life she would continue to show a passion for building a fortune. But Lizzie never did this, living a solitary life with few friends. Her singular crime of violence was directed at only two people, and was never again symbolically reflected in any of her actions. Intense rage exploded out of her like a volcano, never to be repeated. A history of incest could account for this."

The elder Bordens were not just murdered. They were hacked, and hacked, and hacked again. Long after the victims were dead, they were viciously struck over and over. Clearly, the person wielding the ax was doing more than just murdering. That person was experiencing a sheer, frightening, uncontrollable rage. And to be so angry at the victims, the murderer had to have been closely involved with them emotionally. In its heated and passionate vindictiveness, the murder could not have been perpetrated by an "outsider." It was a murder committed by a member of the immediate family – a family member who was viciously angry over something.

19

As we have seen, many aspects of Lizzie's personality and family life fit the pattern of incest. While the theory of incest remains entirely speculative, it would certainly explain the enraged, ferocious manner in which the Bordens were attacked. There is little else, it seems, to account for the terrible, sustained violence with which Lizzie utterly destroyed two human beings.

Primary reference: McNamara, Dr. M. Eileen. "Was Lizzie Borden The Victim of Incest?" In **Rhode Island Medicine,** *February, 1993, Volume 76, p. 95-97.*

THE REAL "CRIMES" OF SALEM'S WITCHES

As 1992 drew to a close, so did the 300th anniversary of a nightmare. The Salem Witch Trials of 1692 have become the stuff of romantic folklore and profitable tourist attractions, and, packaged in these forms, the trials and their disturbing implications have been somewhat sanitized.

In this section, we will avoid the stereotypical hype that ordinarily surrounds discussion of these events, and, instead, we will subject the phenomenon to some urgent inquiry.

Why did intelligent, devout, reasonably educated colonists begin to kill their own sisters, mothers, and daughters? In sociological terms, what does New England witch-hunting tell us about colonial Salem—indeed, about life in all of early colonial Massachusetts?

A modern commentator writes:

> *The story of witchcraft is primarily the story of women...(It) confronts us with ideas about women, with fears about women, with the place of women in society, and with women themselves. It confronts us too with systematic violence against women... (though some men were tried), witches were generally thought of as women and most who died in the name of witchcraft were women.*
>
> Karlsen:xii

The writer goes on to say that "we still live with witches in our culture, however their shape may have changed over time." What does such a statement imply? It seems to suggest that, to some extent, our society is still fearful (and abusive) of women who fail to conform to prevailing societal dictates and "norms" concerning womanhood. To a significant degree, this type of fear also served (albeit unconsciously) to drive 17th-century witch-hunting along its horrific course.

Not all victims of colonial New England witch persecution were female. Yet in non-outbreak witchcraft cases for the years 1620-1725, 83% of accused persons were women, and 94% of people executed for witchcraft were women. In outbreak witchcraft cases of the same period (where accusations were running rampant), men had more to fear, though women were still the foremost targets of witch fear: 76% of accused persons were women, and 77% of people executed as witches were women. These New England statistics have similar correlations in European witch cases of the same period.

An important question arises: what sociological factors made it more likely for women to be subject to witch accusations than men? And even more importantly, were all women in Puritan New England equally prone to such accusations, or were certain "types" of women at greater risk? In addressing these questions, we must first briefly review certain elemental features of Puritan New England social structure and religion.

Puritan life in early colonial New England was markedly hierarchical and rigidly patriarchal. In this distinctly structured society, all people were deemed subordinate to God, though the notion of divinely-ordained hierarchy did not stop here. Puritan religious thought dictated that, in the same manner that all people were subordinate to God, all women were likewise subordinate to men, for the Puritans took the Biblical account of creation quite literally and unimaginatively, using it to justify the patriarchal impulse. The Biblical notion that Eve was created only as an "afterthought" (from Adam's rib, so that he would have a "helpmate") served to reinforce the Puritan belief that God's ordained hierarchy positioned men above women. (Also operative in this attitude were the Biblical epistles of Paul, which, when taken out of their historical context, are easily misinterpreted to endorse female docility.)

The key component of Puritan religious and political thought was the notion of a divinely-ordained social order; that is, men were thought to occupy a position superior to that of women because of a  hierarchical structure which, the Puritans believed, was reflected in the Biblical account of creation and which, ultimately, was the mandate of God Himself.

Within a Puritan context, what would happen if a woman happened to defy this divinely-ordained, hierarchical social order? What if it was not in her nature to be passively quiet, submissive and docile? What if she did not have a supervisory male (i.e. husband) to "keep her in check," sexually and otherwise? God's "well-ordered society," in which the primary role of women was deemed to be that of bearing children and serving as "helpmates" and companions to their husbands, was a crucial component of Puritan thought.

Women who failed to conform to prevailing Puritan notions of womanhood were acutely feared as threats to the existing social order. And, within the context of Puritan society, any woman who was thus feared had much to fear herself; namely, she was prone to accusations of witchcraft. While witch accusations were not exclusively limited to females who did not conform to Puritan standards, such women were by far the most vulnerable, suggesting that witch persecution involved more than mere religious superstition. The disturbing implication is that there was a "method to the madness," and that witch persecution was actually a specific means of social control.

Before presenting statistical evidence to support this position, let us examine two classic cases from the pre-Salem years. The women involved in both accounts were intelligent, outgoing, and respectably self-assertive; they thought for themselves, and they acted (or spoke) on those thoughts. Unfortunately, it was these personal strengths, which would be rightly respected today, that brought these women terrible hardship in early colonial New England.

The case of Ann Hibbens serves to demonstrate the profound dangers to which an assertive, independently spirited woman was subject in Puritan Massachusetts. In 1640, Hibbens publicly complained about the poor quality of work performed for her by two Boston carpenters (who also overcharged her). By standing up for herself against two males (rather than having her husband file the complaint), Hibbens had demonstrated an assertive, independent character that the Puritan authorities apparently found inappropriate. She was brought before the ministers and deacons of the church on charges of "discontent" and "contentiousness." And, because she had argued her case against the two carpenters so well, Governor Winthrop began to outrageously intimate that she was probably also guilty of "sexual seduction," for this would explain how she had developed the verbal skills to argue her point against the carpenters so persuasively! The ministers also charged Hibbens with "great pride of spirit," since she herself had complained about the carpenters, rather than relying on her husband to do it, thereby "usurping (the) authority over him (her husband) whom God hath made her head."

Hibbens was excommunicated by the church, though no accusations of witchcraft were made against her at this time (perhaps because authorities trusted that Ann's husband would henceforth keep her assertiveness in check). However, with the death of her husband in 1654, the Boston widow found herself in immediate danger; her earlier assertiveness had earned her the precarious reputation of having "great pride of spirit," and, as she was no longer living under the authority of a husband, she was now viewed as a threat to the hierarchical social order. Predictably, in 1656, she was formally accused of witchcraft. If her earlier assertiveness had made her seem an aberration, "how much more dangerous she must have appeared by 1656, when she was an economically independent woman living alone" (Karlsen: 152). Puritan authorities dealt with Ann in a most horrifying manner: they deprived her of life by hanging her. Even the prominent minister John Norton conceded that she had been "hanged for a witch, only for having more wit than her neighbors" (Hutchinson: 187).

A more celebrated case is that of Anne Hutchinson, who, while never formally tried for witchcraft, was informally accused of it many times and was eventually banished from both the church and from Massachusetts Bay Colony. Not only did Hutchinson's outspoken theological views contradict many of those held by the orthodox Puritan church, but her presentation of these views violated Pauline (and Puritan) prescriptions against women speaking out on spiritual matters or having any voice in church affairs. By holding (and leading) weekly spiritual meetings, Hutchinson was practicing what male Puritan religious leaders considered to be "blasphemy...(it) evoked images of chaos in the social order...women who assumed to preach God's word called into question not only the hierarchical relations between preacher and hearer but the ordered relations between husband and wife, and magistrate and subject" (Karlsen: 122). Hutchinson was warned by authorities that her assumption of spiritual authority "was not tolerable nor comely in the sight of God nor fitting for your sex" **(Examination of Mrs. Anne Hutchinson: 34)**.

Again, as in the case of Ann Hibbens, we find that female independence and assertiveness were immediately met with suspicions of witchcraft. Governor Winthrop continuously intimated that Hutchinson was a witch; when a woman by the name of Mary Dyer gave birth to a malformed, stillborn infant,

Winthrop attributed the deformity to Hutchinson's witchcraft, since Hutchinson had been present at the birth (Winthrop; 1:268).

The cases of Ann Hibbens and Anne Hutchinson point to a disturbing pattern in New England witchcraft accusations; namely, that such accusations were generally not arbitrary, but were actually directed toward a particular "type" of woman who was deemed to be a threat to the hierarchical, male-dominated Puritan social order. As indicated earlier, the implication is that witch prosecutions in early New England were not merely a haphazard result of religious superstition. Rather, they were a precise and directed means of social control, a social device that was used to suppress, or even eliminate, "undesirable" women. Of course, this was not always the case (some people—including males—were simply accused of witchcraft by neighbors with personal vendettas). But, as the statistics indicate, most cases were not this simple; the majority of accusations reflect a particular pattern of repression—one that was primarily directed toward unconventional women.

What do the statistics tell us? First, while women of all ages were susceptible to accusations, women over forty were the most likely to be tried and convicted. Between 1620 and 1725 only five females under forty were convicted (and just one executed), whereas twenty-seven women over forty were convicted (and seventeen executed) during the same period. Clearly, women over 40 were at much greater risk; again, we see a particular pattern to witch hysteria—one that suggests a certain social component: "...the main targets of witchcraft fears...were almost all over forty. (These) women had reached a point in their lives when they were no longer performing what Puritans considered to be a major role of women: they were no longer bearing children" (Karlsen: 71).

The statistics require further analysis, however. Was it merely because they were not bearing children that these women became socially suspect, or were there other factors involved? An examination of the marital and economic status of witchcraft hunting victims reveals, again, that a particular "type" of woman over forty was especially vulnerable: namely, a woman who was without a husband (either because she was widowed or had never married), and who was economically independent, was most at risk. Why? Because in a society that emphasized female docility and submissiveness, the unmarried, economically independent woman possessed too much liberty to suit Puritan tastes. Her independence made her a threat to the hierarchical, male-dominated social order:

> *It was not merely the absence of a protector that made women alone more susceptible than married women to witchcraft prosecutions. Like their age, the marital status of women was crucial in determining their relationship to their...society. In the eyes of her community, the woman alone in early New England was an aberration: the fundamental female role of procreation was at best irrelevant to her. At worst, of course, she might be performing this function outside the institution of marriage. Moreover, women alone no longer performed—perhaps never performed—the other*

main function of women in New England society: they were not the "helpmates" to men Puritans thought women should be. Even more than women over forty, women alone could not legitimately answer (their end) in (God's) creation.

Karlsen: 75.

While the actual statistics reveal that a significant number of married women were also accused, adjustments must be made for their larger numbers in the total population. Proportionately, it turns out that unmarried women were at greater risk (45 were accused between 1620 and 1725), especially those who were economically independent. Again the implication is that witch prosecution often had a social end: namely, it reflected a societal fear toward independent women whose assertiveness or lack of a male guardian made them seem overtly threatening to the male-dominated social hierarchy. In the end, the Puritans often attacked what they feared, and witch prosecution, to a significant extent, seems to have been just that: an attack on women who failed to conform to Puritan standards. While this attack may not have been a fully conscious one, it was no less deadly for the women involved.

Selected References

Boyer, Paul and Nissembaum, Steven. Salem Possessed: The Social Origins of Witchcraft (Cambridge, Mass., 1974.)

"Church Trial of Mistress Ann Hibbens," in Roots of Bitterness: Documents of the Social History of American Women (New York, 1972, 47-58; Edited by Nancy F. Cott.)

29

"The Examination of Mrs. Anne Hutchinson at the Court of Newtown," in <u>Roots of Bitterness</u> (36-46, see above.)

Hutchinson, Thomas, <u>The History of the Colony and Province of Massachusetts Bay</u> 2 Vols. (London: 1765-68.)

Karlsen, Carol F., <u>The Devil in the Shape of a Woman</u> (Princeton: University of New England Press, 1985.)

Mather, Cotton, <u>The Wonders of the Invisible World</u> (1693; 1862 London Edition.)

Winthrop, John, <u>Winthrop's Journal: "History of New England"</u>, 2 Vols., ed. James Kendall Hosmer (New York: 1908.)

SCAMMED,
CIRCA 1902

At the turn of the century, when rural farming communities were much more common than they are today, New England country towns often attracted an unsavory brand of character: the swindler. As one 1902 book on American crime put it: "Farmers seem to be the legitimate prey of a great army of oily tongued sharks. Swindlers from larger cities penetrate our rural regions, draining it of a large proportion of its wealth, as tribute to cunning frauds, lazy canvassing agents, and downright criminal swindles of all kinds."

Unaccustomed to the vice and corruption so commonplace in America's growing cities, many rural New England folk of the late 19th and 20th centuries were generally more trusting of human character than their urban counterparts. Hence, they sometimes found no reason to question (until it was too late) the integrity of smooth-talking city sophisticates who passed through rural towns touting some elaborate business scheme or another. Of course, as a generally sensible lot, not all farmers were readily taken advantage of. Apparently, however, a good number were, for American crime reports dating to the turn of the century are rife with accounts of frauds that were successfully perpetrated—again and again—on residents of rural farming communities.

If you were living in rural Massachusetts (or any rural New England town) in, say, 1902, what swindles, imported by city sharks from places like Providence or Boston, might you have been subject to? The following descriptions, taken verbatim from E. G. Redmond's 1902 crime study entitled *Frauds of America,* examine the various criminal scams that were perpetrated, with startling frequency, on turn-of-the-century farmers. If nothing else, Mr. Redmond's words—written nearly 100 years ago—should demonstrate that the "idyllic" agrarian past was not as idyllic as we might like to believe. Mr. Redmond's 1902 descriptions are as follows:

Note: To preserve the originality and integrity of the source, Redmond's punctuation, even where incorrect, has been left unaltered.

"A swindle that has been worked repeatedly is to enter town and to offer to purchase a farmer's corn at a certain price per bushel and to get the farmer to sign a contract for delivery of the corn. The swindler has a 'double' fountain pen which is so arranged that it uses two kinds of ink. One ink will eventually fade ('disappearing ink') and the other will remain. The swindler writes out the agreement with the farmer, using the ink that fades. The unsuspecting farmer is then handed the pen to sign his name, but by a turn of a knob the lasting ink has now been made to flow. By this arrangement the words of the contract soon disappear, while the farmer's signature remains. By this time the swindler has departed. He then writes out a promissory note for whatever amount he sees fit above the farmer's signature and then he has the note (cashed) at the farmer's local bank. Many farmers have been swindled in this manner.

There is a species of fraud that farmers should be specially warned against. All farmers are naturally anxious to secure a good price for whatever stock they have to sell. If a seemingly respectable purchaser shows up and offers a little above local market prices, especially if he offers to pay 'on the spot' with a seemingly good cashier's check, the farmer is likely to take up the offer. In such instances, the purchaser just happens to have on his person a cashier's draft for an amount exceeding that of the purchase price of the farmer's stock he wishes to buy. So the farmer pays back 'change'—in actual cash—for the difference and takes the cashier's draft. Later, long after the swindler has departed, the farmer learns that the cashier's draft is a forgery. The difference he paid out as 'change' is good money lost.

Another swindle is often perpetrated on the more superstitious of farmers. Almost every farmer is willing to sell his farm provided he is offered what he considers an attractive amount. A stranger drops in unannounced on the farmer to inquire about purchasing the farm at an appealing price. After being shown carefully over the farm the stranger is invited to remain the night to discuss the deal. But suddenly the stranger is taken ill in the night and remains for four or five days in an apparent stupor, eating lightly, but in reality keeping his eyes and ears wide open. The kind-hearted farmer has too much feeling to put the sick stranger out and nurses and cares for him. When the stranger recovers he informs the farmer that during his illness and while apparently unconscious he dreamed for three nights in succession that he had discovered, in a certain ravine in a remote place on the farm, an earthen jar buried in the ground, containing a large amount of silver. At this the farmer usually expresses surprise and refers to it as a most mysterious dream. The stranger suggests they walk over the farm in the section covered by the dream, and the farmer's curiosity is sharpened, and 'just for fun' to see if there is anything to such dreams, gets a shovel and digs for the hidden treasure. A rock is struck, the dirt carefully removed, and when the rock is lifted there is revealed a large earthen jar brimming full of silver shining dollars. It is quietly carried to the house and the farmer thinks an equal division would be fair. There is usually from ten to twelve hundred silver dollars in one of these 'finds.' The stranger asks the farmer if he would give him a check for his half, or get paper currency for him, as the silver is too much of a load for him to carry. The farmer is, of course, willing to do anything for his new 'friend.' After the stranger leaves, promising that he will think over the purchase of the farm and will soon call again, the farmer finds too late that he has been cleverly swindled, for the 'silver' is nothing more than a plated composition of some worthless metal that was secretly buried by the stranger before his arrival. The stranger, of course, hurriedly cashes the farmer's check, leaves town, and is never seen again.

Another favorite mode of swindling that is meeting with a measure of success is for rascal No. 1 to call on a farmer and make a contract of the purchase of the farm at a stipulated price, and gives him $50 or $100, as the case may be, to bind the bargain. In due time a confederate, rascal No. 2, calls upon the farmer and offers him a third more or double the contract figures, and expresses much regret when the farmer tells him the farm is under contract already. After stewing over the matter for several days, visiting the farm again and again, and *making mysterious explorations into ravines and gullies, as if to demonstrate a keen interest in the property, rascal No. 2 confidentially suggests that the farmer go quietly to the first man who put down the deposit on the property, and buy him off so as to make a new contract at a far higher price. This the farmer usually does, giving the first man from $500 to $1000 bonus to release him. Of course, rascal No. 2 then never calls again, for he and rascal No. 1 were working together. It is a cleverly worked swindle, pure and simple.*

There is always a great outcry in rural communities against well-dressed, plausible, traveling swindlers, who secure the signatures of unsuspecting farmers on a slip of paper ostensibly to secure the prompt payment, on delivery, for some horse-rake, pump, plow, or other article, offered for sale at a very low price, and on very easy terms, at some future time. On these slips of paper they have the signature written in such a position that they can easily fill out a promissory note for any amount, and the victimized farmers soon afterwards find these notes in circulation with their names attached. To all of our readers we have to give the often repeated advice: give such rascals a wide berth, and never sign anything for a stranger.

The most contemptible individual known to modern farmers is the traveling quack doctor. He steals into a rural community with his advertising material. He inquires who is sick and makes personal canvass. Sometimes he employs some member of the community more contemptible than himself to go with him and introduce and recommend him. He finds some individual suffering from one of the many ills that beset us all and tells of the great number of cases of this kind that have *been cured by him, and that notwithstanding the case has baffled the skill of the local physicians it is a very simple case for him, and if he doesn't cure he will refund all money. People who are afflicted with disease are ready to respond to any proposition that will relieve the weary, oppressed body. Fifty or $100.00 they consider a slight remuneration to a man with skill sufficient to effect a cure and they quickly sign a promissory note for that amount or more. The quack doctor's promise of 'refund if no cure' is not incorporated into the note and the eminent doctor, as soon as he secures the note, considers his work ended and quickly leaves town.*

There are a thousand and one schemes for entrapping the unwary farmer, but if he is caught napping in any transaction he has only himself to blame. Let strangers alone, and only deal with reputable houses. Give all questionable transactions a wide berth, sign nothing unless you know that it is legitimate and in any deal that necessitates a money transaction consult your local banker."

*All above excerpts from Redmond, E. G., **Frauds of America** (1902)*

CHAPTER TWO

NEW ENGLAND AFTER DARK:

GHOSTS AND VAMPIRES

HORRIFIC HAUNTING AT REHOBOTH'S VILLAGE CEMETERY

Rehoboth's Village Cemetery, located in Rehoboth Village, Massachusetts, is the purported site of an allegedly true and unsettling ghostly manifestation. In researching the case, I have interviewed five different witnesses to the apparition, all of whom were carefully screened for veracity, sincerity, and well-groundedness. The witnesses involved are intelligent, educated (three of the five have college degrees), long-time Rehoboth residents who, in relating the details of their encounters, exhibited marked emotional effect (i.e. something clearly happened at the cemetery to powerfully upset them).

The first alleged sighting of the Village Cemetery phenomenon purportedly occurred on January 17th, 1994. Daniel and Barbara Miles (pseudonyms to protect privacy) were standing at the center of the cemetery, visiting a relative's grave, when suddenly, in a spot at the southwest rear of the graveyard where there had been no one present just a moment earlier, an elderly man, dressed in old clothing, made an appearance. Daniel and Barbara observed that the man, who had a prominent hooked nose and a sneering facial expression, was curiously kneeling on the ground next to a gravestone. He seemed to be praying and alternately sobbing and laughing. After less than a minute, the bizarre figure suddenly dematerialized, and Barbara and Daniel hurried out of the cemetery in a state of alarm.

Both witnesses claim to have been powerfully upset by the apparitional manifestation (Barbara complains of nightmares about the experience to the present day), and neither has been able to return to the Village Cemetery, despite the fact that a relative is buried there. Neither Daniel nor Barbara has any idea who or what they witnessed on that winter afternoon in 1994. Daniel indicates that whatever it was, it will "upset both (of us) for the rest of our lives."

The second report of the apparition, provided by Lisa and Karen Mackey (sisters and long-time Rehoboth residents), is in many ways similar to the first, even though Lisa and Karen claim that they have no knowledge of the Miles couple and allege—very believably, in this researcher's opinion—that they have never heard anything of the previous couple's experience.

On August 20 or 21 of 1995, Lisa and Karen visited the cemetery to pay respects to their mother, who has been buried there since 1966. The cemetery, they indicate, was completely empty of other people at the time of their visit (about 4:20 P.M.), and they spent approximately 20 minutes at their mother's gravesite. Suddenly, as they prepared to depart, the sisters were startled by a strange sound deriving from the southwestern rear portion of the graveyard (the precise location where the Miles couple had earlier seen the apparitional old man). The sound was that of human whistling, except, in this case, it was loud, aggressive, erratic and rapid, punctuated by suggestive noises (of the sort made by coarse men and directed at attractive women). When Lisa and Karen looked in that direction, they were startled to see a strange-looking elderly man (their physical description of the man matches that of the Miles couple precisely) staring at them intently and making an obscene gesture with his hands.

The sisters indicate that what startled them most, even more than the inappropriate hand gestures, was the fact that the odd figure standing at the back of the graveyard was clearly not natural. Not only did he move in a strange sort of floating slow motion (a phenomenon reported in numerous other unrelated cases I have researched), but the old man's eyes seemed entirely black and hollow, like two black sockets completely devoid of any eyes at all, as though he was "without the spark of life, somehow soul-less," as Lisa puts it, for lack of a more concrete description.

"The manifestation appeared to us for less than thirty seconds, and then it vanished," adds Karen, " but that's all it took for us to realize that we had glanced upon something that was supernatural and, without question, was also something very evil or, if not evil, then at least very tormented."

The sisters, both of whom were profoundly and understandably shaken and disturbed by the momentary vision in the cemetery, report that they (like the Miles couple) have not yet been able to muster the courage to return to visit their mother's grave— an unfortunate situation.

The final sighting of the old man purportedly took place recently, in the spring (April 4, 6, or 7; that's the best the witness can narrow down the prospective day) of 1996.

"What I (encountered) that day has affected every aspect of my life," observes (pseudonym) Sarah Dickerman, the 36-year-old witness and schoolteacher (Taunton). "I pray that you (i.e. the author/interviewer) can help me to understand and come to terms with what I saw, (though) I doubt I ever really will."

Sarah's spring 1996 encounter with the apparitional old man at Village Cemetery is in many ways the most frightening report of all, especially considering that—unlike the other witnesses to the manifestation—she was entirely alone at the time and has been forced, at least until our recent series of interviews, to struggle with her experience entirely on her own.

Sarah indicates that while taking a walk through the cemetery for relaxation, she reportedly observed an elderly man at the southwestern rear part of the graveyard, kneeling on the ground and sobbing. (Not only does the location and physical description of the man correlate with the two previous accounts, but the

kneeling and sobbing is a phenomenon that the Miles couple also allegedly witnessed.) Before she had a chance to fully note the man's unnatural appearance, Sarah assumed he was a distraught mourner and began to approach to offer comfort. When she came to within a few yards of the strange character, she indicates, he suddenly sprang to his feet (in retrospect, says Sarah, with a type of "liquid" movement that wasn't natural), and then he burst out in strange laughter. A second later, he called Sarah a "(expletive)" directly to her face. Profoundly startled, Sarah quickly turned away and began to walk briskly in the direction of her parked car. The bizarre old man, she says, began to follow her, and behind her she could hear him alternately laughing and then loudly and inexplicably yelling, "Catherine, Catherine, you (expletive)!" although the woman's name, of course, wasn't Catherine. At that point, in a state of pronounced panic, Sarah broke into a terrified run toward her car, which was parked on the road to the side of the cemetery. Upon reaching her vehicle, she was astonished to observe, in the distance, that the old man had re-materialized back in his original spot at the southwestern rear part of the cemetery. He had inexplicably relocated over an impossible distance in just a matter of seconds. As she nervously began to drive away, the astonished woman noticed from her car window that the bizarre old man was now leaning over and beating with his fists a young woman lying prostrate before him on the ground. A moment later, both figures entirely vanished. (This is the first instance in which there was a hint of a second ghost's involvement in the haunting—possibly the 'Catherine' to which the apparition had earlier referred.)

Does this horrifying Village Cemetery haunting involve some terrible human drama/conflict that is re-enacting itself over and over again in the cemetery—on some spectral, alternate—dimensional plane that is only discernible/observable to a certain select few "sensitive" observers and not to most of us? Does this alternate plane occasionally somehow superimpose itself, under certain unknown conditions, on our present reality? Or, do all of the witnesses—despite their convincing sincerity and authentic emotional affect—really know each other, thus rendering the separate accounts "copy-cat" sightings?

I merely raise these controversial questions and make no profession of belief in such things. I, like most of you, do not begin to understand, though I must say that the witnesses in question were, as indicated, thoughtful, credible people who had no reason to fabricate their accounts (which remained consistent throughout multiple comprehensive interviews).

ANOTHER REHOBOTH HAUNTING: WHAT LURKS ON LAKE ST.?

It is a crisp, windy fall evening. The moon—peering through the skeletal treetops like a pale china doll—casts a pallid white glow over the tiny, timeworn graveyard. Amidst the moldering tombstones, jagged dead leaves stir from the ground and rise up in the wind, filling the air with dark, swirling shadows in the shapes of mad, twisted angels.

I penned the above lines while visiting—on a moonlit, chilly autumn eve last year—the Palmer River Burying Ground on Lake Street, in Rehoboth, Massachusetts. I was there with two friends at about midnight, skeptically hoping to spot a Lake Street ghost I had heard about. I was carrying a pad to record any unusual observations, and—while my friends and I never did encounter any ghosts—I felt strongly inclined to catch the eerie mood of the place in writing. Ghosts or no ghosts, the decrepit, two-century-old Palmer River Burying Ground—late on a moonlit night—sends a shudder up your spine that settles in your throat like a lump of cold lead.

But the question remains: is this old Burying Ground haunted? I myself cannot say, for I have been researching the place for the past three years, and I have yet to bump into any dead folk on Lake Street. Until I do, a part of me must remain at least somewhat skeptical. I must say, however, that of all the old cemeteries in Rehoboth, Lake Street's Palmer River Burying Ground is by far the most frequently cited when people approach me with reports of ghostly graveyard encounters.

The old-timers in town might ask: why have we not heard anything about Lake Street's ghosts until now? Well, one possible explanation is that in years past, there were no available venues for reporting an alleged ghost sighting. More recently, however, with the publication of various Rehoboth ghost reports in my recent book, *The New England Ghost Files* (Covered Bridge Press—1994), many local residents seem less reluctant to talk about such experiences, and there is presently a sympathetic researcher on the scene (namely, myself) with whom they can openly discuss their encounters.

Hence, ghostly encounters that just a few years ago would have gone unreported are now entering the public record, and a new body of Rehoboth folklore (is it merely folklore?) is gradually evolving. As indicated earlier, the Palmer River Burying Ground figures prominently in this new body of local ghost lore.

Following are a few ghostly encounters involving this very old cemetery—some recent, others that purportedly took place years ago. (As always, names and identifying personal characteristics might be slightly altered—where requested—to assure privacy and anonymity):

July 21, 1983: A 56 year-old woman and her 27 year-old daughter, both Rehoboth residents who lived near the Lake Street vicinity, allegedly observed an apparition in the cemetery while walking their dogs along Lake Street.

The older woman reports: "It was an hour before sunset, and as we got near the cemetery, we both saw a simple black casket

45

lying at the edge of the graveyard. This was very odd, because we both knew that the cemetery had not been used for burials for more than a century. We moved toward the cemetery for a closer look, but then we noticed—to our (astonishment)—that the casket was now gone. It had completely disappeared before our eyes. What was really weird…well, after the casket vanished, for a few moments after that my daughter and I heard (distinct) singing coming from the middle of the graveyard, even though there was nobody there at the time. It lasted only several seconds or so. It was a man's voice singing a loud, sad song that sounded Irish." (The woman's daughter—a veterinarian now practicing in Maine—confirms her mother's curious account.)

July 7, 1968: A 47-year-old Rehoboth resident, a building contractor, was visiting the cemetery out of historical interest after learning that the town's first meeting house once stood next to the site. His wife was present with him. Both husband and wife report that while at the eastern edge of the cemetery, they suddenly noticed that a small boy had appeared out of nowhere. He was standing approximately ten feet away from them, staring at them intently. The boy wore a simple, very large white shirt that came down to his knees. He was wearing no trousers, and the lower part of his bare leg (left) was noticeably disfigured and deformed.

The couple reported that they were alarmed by the boy's odd appearance and made an attempt to communicate. The husband indicates that the boy contorted his mouth strangely and made no reply, although the wife does not recall this unusual facial expression. Both husband and wife state that, about seven seconds after they attempted to talk to the boy, the child turned away and began to walk in a westward direction. At this point, both husband and wife report becoming extremely frightened, as the boy's gait appeared entirely unnatural. While walking away from them, the child's feet would sometimes touch the ground, but at other times both feet seemed to float several inches above the ground while the boy still moved forward. The husband reports that the boy's curious movement resembled "the Apollo moon walk." He says the gait was "completely normal for a few steps, then (abnormal) as he floated a step or two forward, then normal again as he resumed walking on the ground. It (alternated) back and forth." The boy reached the far edge of the cemetery, stopped, and then inexplicably kicked the ground three times as though angry. Then, he vanished. Both husband and wife report hurriedly leaving the graveyard in a state of semi-panic.

*Note: In June of 1992, there was another alleged sighting of a young boy in the graveyard. The witness—who presented her account very sincerely and thoughtfully—was a single woman, Phillis Hask, as reported in my 1994 book, **The New England Ghost Files** (Covered Bridge Press—1994).*

Interestingly, other visitors to the cemetery have reported hearing the disembodied giggling of a young child (reported as sounding like a boy), even though there was no child visibly present in the graveyard when the giggling was heard.

January 14, 1989: Two Rehoboth women and one Somerset woman—three friends who enjoy doing historical gravestone rubbings—purportedly experienced a bizarre encounter in the

47

graveyard. While all three women were at the central part of the cemetery bending over a grave stone to examine its inscription, they suddenly heard a loud male voice—seemingly speaking out from directly behind them—utter the nonsensical phrase, "Carriage, they never sent, poor, poor." As the startled women swung around to confront the speaker, however, they found no one behind them, and the unidentified voice ceased its incoherent rambling.

As the three perplexed women stood there discussing the bizarre occurrence, they suddenly noticed two men and a small boy standing some distance away—at the edge of the cemetery. Each standing figure was positioned to the left side of a gravestone—three consecutive gravestones in a row—and each stood rigidly upright and motionless, with arms straight down to their sides. Both the men and the boy were staring coldly across the graveyard directly at the three women. And then, just a few moments after the women had first noticed them, the three strange figures became blurry in appearance and then suddenly vanished. The two adult males had been wearing heavy, black clothes. The three women do not specifically recall the attire worn by the young boy, though they indicate that it was much lighter in color than that of the two men.

Note: Was the young boy the same boy who was observed in the two earlier reported incidents? His age and general description—as described by the three women—are in some ways consistent with the other accounts. This last report is the only sighting at the cemetery in which the ghostly boy—rather than appearing alone—has been seen in the company of spectral adults.

CONCLUSIONS—What are we to make of all of this? I myself am not quite sure. I can only attest to the fact that the witnesses I interviewed, all of whom seemed credible and rational, related the details of their reports with consistency and seeming sincerity. All of them seemed strongly affected by their experiences.

Although the details of the various accounts differ markedly, most (although not all) of the Palmer River Burying Ground reports seem to contain a common element: namely—the presence of a young boy, either via visual appearance or via auditory (e.g. the disembodied giggling) manifestation. Somehow—if the cemetery is, in fact, haunted—a troubled youth from Rehoboth's distant past may play a central role.

THE STRANGE CASE OF DR. SPECK

For horrific accounts of the supernatural, one of our most colorful sources is Native American folklore. To the New England Algonquin, the forest has always been a dark and haunted place; a place where ghostly silver faces might suddenly appear in streams; a place where unnameable, glistening black THINGS coil and writhe inside of rotting logs; a place where centuries-old witches might be sitting in the treetops unnoticed...watching...waiting for you....

The following tale is Mohegan and derives from Connecticut. It dates to the early part of this century.

In the late 1930's, a highly-trained, well-respected anthropologist named Dr. Frank G. Speck began an ethnology project in Connecticut. More specifically, he set out to study and record Mohegan Indian myths and legends, including Mohegan ghost lore. Naturally, Dr. Speck fully believed that none of these myths and legends were actually true. He merely wished to record and preserve the stories as part of his cultural ethnology project.

And then, around 1940, something rather unexpected happened. While conducting his studies in a rural part of Connecticut, Dr. Speck allegedly encountered one of the "mythical" Mohegan ghosts in question! That is, he claimed to have *observed the ghost first-hand!* For the first time in the history of social science, a highly-trained and well-respected anthropologist was claiming that he had directly interfaced with a living dead person!

Dr. Speck related his bizarre experience to a close acquaintance—a Wampanoag writer who recorded the incident after Speck's death in 1950. Clearly, Dr. Speck had been powerfully affected by the experience, for why else would he have risked career and reputation by talking about it to anyone?

The following original account was written by the Wampanoag in whom Dr. Speck had confided. This obscure document first appeared in a typed newsletter circulated by the Federated East Indian League sometime around 1960; more recently, it appeared in a book by William S. Simmons, Professor of Anthropology at the University of California, Berkeley. The account reads as follows:

"The late and beloved Dr. Frank G. Speck, who spent his life working as an ethnologist and an organizer among the Indian Tribes of the east, once related to me one of his strangest and most unforgettable experiences. He said that as is the manner of many college-trained students, he listened to superstitious stories as related to him by Indian friends, but that he certainly did not believe in them; that is, until when one time something happened that was to change his whole viewpoint about Indian ghost stories.

Dr. Speck had gone up to do some field work among the Mohegan Indians who live at Mohegan Hill in the village of Uncasville, Connecticut. He was having supper with a Mohegan couple with whom he had spent the day taking notes on folklore and herbal lore. It had been a pleasant day, and they had rambled through the woods in the old Mohegan settlement, and he worked up quite an appetite. I believe that

51

the name of the couple was Cooper, and as she was preparing a big supper Indian style with corn bread, succotash, Indian Pudding and pork sausage, Dr. Speck said that as he looked out the window he could see the orange moon beginning to rise through the treetops. 'Oh look', he said, 'There is going to be a beautiful full moon tonight.' As he said this, he said that the man looked at his wife and said something in a low voice that was not intended for Dr. Speck to hear. He noticed this but said nothing.

When supper was ready, Dr. Speck and the Coopers sat down to a hearty meal and really enjoyed themselves. After the meal they got up and sat down around the kitchen stove and relaxed with the good smell of woodsmoke, and Dr. Speck lit up a cigar. He was so relaxed he said that he did not notice the time, and when he looked at his watch he said that it was time for him to go back to Cynthia Fowler's house. The lady looked at Dr. Speck in a strange way and said that she and her husband thought it best that he remain with them for the night. Dr. Speck replied that since Cynthia would be expecting him he thought that he should be on his way. Both husband and wife then looked at each other strangely and seemed to be sort of embarrassed. Dr. Speck then spoke up and asked if there was something wrong. The woman stopped rocking in her chair and looked at Dr. Speck directly and said, 'Dr. Speck, the old Indian Stone Cutter will be working tonight!' He looked at the woman relieved and said, 'Well that's all right with me. I don't mind if he's working tonight, and I can understand if he has so much work to do during the day that at night he might have to work over to finish up his chores.' The woman and her husband looked again at each other, and it was then that Dr. Speck knew by their glances that something was really wrong.

Finally the man spoke up and said, 'Dr. Speck, the old Indian Stone Cutter has been dead for over 30 years, and when the moon is full he comes out to work and you will have to pass right by the quarry where he works and you will be sure to hear him. We think you had better stay with us tonight.' The Dr. did not wish to hurt their feelings by telling that he did not believe in such things, but he decided to be tactful about the matter. 'Now don't you folks worry,' he began, 'if anything goes wrong I will let you know tomorrow, but I will be all right!' He bade them both good night and started out through the woods whistling. As he came close to the quarry, he felt strange and stopped for a moment. The chink, chink sound of someone cutting stone was coming from the quarry. Dr. Speck said to himself, 'Oh, that is just my imagination playing tricks upon me.' He started to walk again and the closer he came to the quarry, the louder the sound of stone cutting became. He thought to himself, I will go see who is out cutting stone at this hour. Finally as he walked closer to the sound, and as it became louder he could see no one in sight though the moon was nice and clear. Suddenly the sound stopped and he felt relieved and knew that it was only his imagination. He breathed a sigh of relief, but suddenly the sound commenced again, and this time it was directly in back of him. He wheeled around and saw no one, and then he decided to move. He ran through the woods and the sound followed him and he never stopped until he was back at the Cooper home. He bolted in the door, and there was a note on the table by the lamp. It said, 'We knew that you would be back. Your bed is all turned down. See you in the morning.' He went right to bed, but said that he could not forget how those sounds followed him through the woods. From that moment on, whenever the Indian people gave

53

him advice or told him about some haunted place to stay away from, Dr. Frank G. Speck never made light of their superstitions, and if they advised him not to go to this place or that place, he heeded them.

Hearing the old Mohegan Indian Stone Cutter had made him a changed man."

(As reprinted in *Spirit of the New England Tribes*. Simmons, Dr. William S. -University Press of New England—1966:144.)

This curious account represents the only known instance in which a white New England anthropologist reported an actual encounter with a "mythical" Native American ghost. Such things have allegedly been experienced by two or three anthropologists working with western tribes, but Dr. Speck's experience is unique to the annals of New England anthropological studies.

The more skeptical among us might ask: were some mischievous Indians playing a joke on Dr. Speck, maybe hiding themselves in the quarry and producing the sounds themselves? Perhaps, but we must keep in mind that Dr. Speck was a highly intelligent and educated man, and that he probably wouldn't have given the incident a second thought unless he had already ruled out the possibility of a hoax. Certainly, he wouldn't have risked career and reputation by talking about his experience unless he was absolutely convinced that the encounter was supernatural in nature. And besides, how was it that the phantom sounds followed Speck through the woods as he ran back to the Cooper house? A few mischievous Indians hiding down in a quarry wouldn't have been able to pull off a stunt like that.

Of course, even the most intelligent and educated of scientists are only human; on a dark, eerie night, anyone's imagination can go into overdrive. Yet, with anthropologists who are trained to be entirely empirical and objective about the cultural data they are studying, it is extraordinarily rare for a skilled ethnologist to become a believer of the myths and legends he is studying.

The case remains unexplained.

RHODE ISLAND AFTER DARK

Introductory Note: The following article discusses some of the cultural components that gave rise to early New England Vampire legends of the sort presented in the next two articles that follow this one.

Back then, it wasn't known as the "Ocean State." Far from it. In fact, newspapers of the 1890's dubbed Rhode Island the "Transylvania of the Western World" and "Vampire Capital of America." And, although these names, even today, might still be fitting when we think about a Rhode Island politician or two, in the 1890's Rhode Island's alleged "vampires" were not blood-sucking elected officials but rather real, true-to-life creatures of the darkness—undead, diabolical beings who stalked the state's moonlit, shadowy countryside in search of weary nighttime travelers whose souls were ripe for the picking.

Well, sort of. In reality, of course, there were no immortal, blood-lusting demons lurking in the shadows and cemeteries of Rhode Island (with the exception, perhaps, of a few Rhode Island politicians, even back then). However, between 1870 and 1900, such dark entities did, indeed, lurk in the minds and beliefs of many Rhode Islanders—especially the country folk of rural South County.

For one thing, the isolated country villages of South County (Coventry, Exeter, East & West Greenwich, etc.) physically resembled the lonely hamlets of Transylvania. This topographical similarity inspired some Eastern European immigrants to Rhode Island to recall (and culturally transplant) many vampire legends from the old country.

For another thing, throughout the second half of the 19th-century, South County was prone to acute epidemics of tuberculosis (particularly the variety known as "consumption," which settled in the lungs). As more and more young, previously healthy people were suddenly and inexplicably swept away by the strange disease (whose etiology was unknown to most country doctors of the period), confused villagers sought explanations for (and thereby control of) the mysterious phenomenon.

The explanation they came up with was that of vampirism: late night visitations by one of the living dead, who would, it was believed, materialize in the bedroom of a young, healthy person (usually a person who had been, in life, the once-human vampire's immediate sibling or relative), sucking the life out of the victim by sitting or lying atop the sleeping person's body night after night, until the person weakened and eventually died, also becoming a vampire who would itself soon lurk in the nighttime shadows of the family farmhouse, attacking its own siblings/relatives as they slept. (Consumptive tuberculosis was often a family disease, spread by close contact within the farmhouse, as well as by a hereditary component.)

At the disease's peak (1870-1900), such beliefs gave rise to numerous vampire hunts and corpse exhumations throughout rural Rhode Island. The dead bodies of suspected vampires were unearthed and examined for signs of continued activity within the grave—i.e. scratch marks on the inside of the coffin lid—as well as for continued physical growth after death and burial, such as "longer" hair and nails and fresh-looking blood within the corpse. (In fact, such oddly well-preserved corpses were encountered quite frequently, though usually by over-emotional and imaginative family members who had buried the deceased only recently, perhaps in the frozen ground of winter.)

If an exhumed "vampire" could be conclusively identified, villagers believed, it could be killed "again" via the removal and burning of its heart or liver (depending on which organ still contained fresh blood—another "sure sign" of the deceased person's vampirism). After the organ was burned, surviving family members, in a strange ritual that probably derived from Eastern Europe, often consumed the ashes, sometimes by mixing them into the medicine of sick but still-living family members. Then, the body of the "vampire" was reburied. Subsequent to the ritual, the body could supposedly no longer leave the grave at night to stalk its remaining human relatives.

What is a vampire? Historian Nancy Kinder, in *Mysterious New England* (Yankee Books), notes that "the vampire is considered to be a type of undead spirit. Legend presumes it to be a living corpse which comes from its burial place to drink the blood of the living." Webster's dictionary further defines the vampire as "a reanimated corpse that rises from the grave at night to suck the blood of sleeping persons." Finally, Rhode Island historian Donald Boisvert suggests that the vampire is best defined as "a walking corpse without a soul, driven by a thirst for blood...(or) vampires may be the souls of the dead which come out of the tomb by night and prey upon the blood of the living, usually that of relatives."

While the vampire, throughout the ages, may have been all of these things, it was, in this writer's opinion, also something else. The vampire was, in certain contexts, a cultural strategy.

At a time when science offered no immediate solution to the problem of rural tuberculosis, Rhode Island's South County villagers creatively afforded themselves at least some sense of control by putting a "face" on the enemy. In this place and time, disease-causing genes and germs could not be seen, hunted, and destroyed. But vampires could be. Like the folklore of other cultures, the vampire myths of South County's villagers allowed them to unconsciously create an illusion of control over an uncontrollable disease and thereby curb feelings of utter helplessness and fear. To the people who chased vampires, then, the enemy was very real.

Hence, as consumptive tuberculosis spread over the countryside, vampire hunts and corpse exhumation in late 19th-century South County became, as indicated, countless in number. So many cases were reported in the press that Rhode Island, as noted earlier, earned the dubious distinction of "Vampire Capital of America."

The pages (circa 1870-1900) of such publications as *The Narragansett Times* and *The Providence Journal* contain numerous recorded references to vampire-related activity in and around rural South County.

Two of Rhode Island's more famous true cases of alleged "vampirism" follow in the next two articles.

THE WORDS ON
NELLY'S TOMBSTONE

*Note: The following article was first published by Mr. Robinson in the March, 1994 issue of **Yankee**.*

The villagers of Exeter, Rhode Island, knew that farmer George Brown had a problem. First, in 1883, his wife, Mary, succumbed to a mysterious illness. Six months later, his 20-year-old daughter, Mary Olive, also fell ill and died. Within the next several years, his 19-year-old daughter, Mercy, was also dead, and George's teenage son Edwin, a healthy lad who worked as a store clerk, became suddenly frail and sick. The village doctor informed George that "Consumption" was taking his family. But the country folk of Exeter had another explanation.

On a chilly March afternoon in 1892, a group of men entered Exeter's Chestnut Hill Cemetery. There they began to exhume the bodies of George Brown's wife and two daughters. They had concluded that one of the deceased was leaving the grave at night to suck the life out of its relatives. Only by killing the vampire could young Edwin be saved.

First, the men examined the bodies of Mrs. Brown and daughter Mary. Finding them to be properly decomposed, they began to exhume Mercy Brown. Slowly, they shoveled into Mercy's grave. When they reached the corpse, the men suddenly stepped back in terror.

Mercy, who had been buried for more than two months, appeared oddly well preserved. It seemed that her hair and nails had grown. And when the men cautiously prodded the corpse with their shovel, they found that it was filled with fresh blood. The suspected vampire's heart was removed and burned on a nearby rock. The ashes were added to young Edwin's medicine. Still, the boy died less than two months later.

To the less superstitious, there was perhaps nothing so unusual about the well-preserved condition of Mercy's body. She had been in the ground during the two coldest months of the year. The mysterious wave of illness that swept George Brown's family was probably tuberculosis.

But that did not keep Rhode Island from becoming known as the "Vampire Capital of America." South County, whose isolated villages resembled the lonely hamlets of Transylvania, was a hotbed of vampire rumors between 1870 and 1900. When Bram Stoker, who wrote *Dracula* in 1897, died, newspaper accounts of Mercy Brown were found in his files.

The legends persist to this day. Until very recently, in Rhode Island Historical Cemetery No. 2 stood the gravestone of alleged vampire Nelly L. Vaughn of West Greenwich, who died in 1889 at the age of 19. The grave is supposedly cursed. One local university professor who studies vampirism claims that "no vegetation or lichen would grow on Nelly's grave," despite numerous attempts to plant there. And people were often taken aback by the inscription along the bottom of Nelly's tombstone. The curious words read... *"I am waiting and watching for you."*

THE VAMPIRE LEGEND OF SNUFFY STUKELEY

Early America was rife with blood-curdling legends. Of the many ghosts and hellish creatures that stalked the colonial imagination, vampires were the most diabolical. Frightful tales of these blood-lusting demons circulated in most towns of the 17th, 18th, and 19th-centuries.

Noah Webster, noting the powerful presence of vampires in early American folklore, included them in his monumental dictionary of 1828. His classic definition described them as "blood-sucking ghosts or reanimated bodies of dead persons believed to come from the grave and wander about by night sucking the blood of a person asleep." Asleep? Who could have slept in those years of nightmarish lore?

In colonial days, New England had its own share of "undead" inhabitants, or so, at least, went local legend. There was an oft-told tale (now almost forgotten) concerning one Snuffy Stukeley, who supposedly owned a large farm in a rural part of Rhode Island in the early 18th-century. The following account, which some believed had basis in fact, is just one of several differing versions of this Rhode Island legend:

Life had been good to Snuffy. His wife had borne him fourteen children, and his farm had been equally fruitful. One night, however, Snuffy received an ominous omen in the form of a dream, and his life would be forever changed.

According to the account, the farmer dreamt of an orchard, one much like the actual orchard on his property. In the dream, exactly one half of the orchard's trees were withered and dead, while the remaining half appeared healthy and lush. When he awoke, Snuffy puzzled over the possible symbolic meaning of the strange vision. He sensed that it portended some tragedy.

A few days later, the farmer's eldest daughter, Sarah, sickened and perished. She was buried in the family cemetery, and shortly thereafter another of Snuffy's daughters became sick. This child's illness was accompanied by something quite odd. She complained that her dead sister was making nighttime visits to her bedroom.

"Sarah comes to my room every night," said the girl. "She sits on different parts of my body and makes me hurt badly."

At first, the child's astonished parents attributed the visions to delirium. Soon, however, the young girl was dead, and a nightmarish pattern began to unfold.

One by one, goes the legend, Snuffy's children sickened and died, until a tragic total of seven of his fourteen youngsters had perished. Before dying, each sick child also complained of painful nightly visits from Sarah. Soon, the farmer and his wife began to suspect the worst: Sarah had become a vampire, and her demonic spirit was making nightly journeys to the Stukeley household, where she was sucking out the lives of her brothers and sisters.

There was just one way to put an end to Sarah's ghastly nighttime visits. Only then could the lives of the seven remaining children be saved. One cold and windy night, with lanterns and shovels in hand, Snuffy and several of his neighbors solemnly ventured into the small cemetery where Sarah had been buried.

Cautiously, the men approached Sarah's grave. With a raw sort of terror pulsing through them, they commenced to dig up her coffin. The grave was soon opened, and the trembling men hoisted the coffin out of the ground. They removed the nails and slowly, ever so slowly, began to lift the lid...

Nothing could have prepared the farmers for the horrific sight now before them. Sarah's corpse was in a most fiendish state. Her eyes were wide open, staring oddly. Her hair and nails had grown to unnatural lengths. When one of the men prodded the body with his shovel, the girl's blood-red lips curled into a demoniacal grin. She was alive! Sarah had become a vampire.

According to this version of the legend, Snuffy proceeded to remove his daughter's heart. As her black blood spattered onto the horrified men, the vampire gave out a blood-curdling shriek, and her hellish eyes rolled wildly. Then, the body became lifeless and still. Alas the ordeal was over, and at that very moment Snuffy thought he heard Sarah's sweet voice in the wind: "I am free. Thank you, dear Daddy, and good-bye for now."

The farmer's prophetic dream of the half-dead, half-living orchard had been fulfilled. Half of his fourteen children were

65

dead. The remaining seven would go on to lead healthy and prosperous lives.

And so goes this particular version of the legend of Snuffy Stukeley and his daughter, the vampire. Generations ago, this curious talk struck terror into the hearts of many New Englanders. In our own enlightened times, legends of this sort have ceased to be frightening. Unflinchingly, any of us could walk alone past some shadowy cemetery late at night. But running, we might tell ourselves, would be much better exercise....

THREE AUTHENTIC HAUNTINGS

Introductory Note: The three accounts presented below took place many years ago, but they were formally researched by the present author fairly recently—with his usual cautious approach. Witnesses were selected for their apparent sincerity, well-groundedness, and reliability. Names and dates may be slightly altered where necessary to protect privacy and anonymity.

Since the author is based in Rehoboth, Massachusetts, most of his recent research for this book involves alleged incidents in this locale. For additional accounts involving all parts of New England, see the author's 1994 critically acclaimed best-seller, *The New England Ghost Files,* which has been called the most credible and unsettling book in its genre by publications like *Yankee* and *The Boston Globe.*

1) Alleged Incident Date—Ca. 1969:
Mr. and Mrs. Joseph Holland, residents of Rehoboth, Massachusetts, and both certified public accountants, report a bizarre occurrence at Rehoboth's Perryville Dam/Pond. While taking a sunset walk at the pond in the summer of 1969, the couple encountered a middle-aged man sitting near the dam, holding his bleeding left foot in his hands. When asked by the couple what had happened, the man indicated that he had been bitten on the foot by a large snapping turtle. The couple began to walk toward a nearby house to call for help, and then turned back toward the man to ask him one last question about his condition. Suddenly, they were astonished to observe that the

man had completely vanished without any natural explanation. In retrospect, the couple says that the man's clothing looked like something from the previous century.

Six other persons (allegedly including a police officer), over the course of the next year, also reportedly encountered an injured man sitting at Perryville Pond/Dam holding a bloody left foot in his hands. In each instance, the man claimed that he had been bitten by a snapping turtle. In all cases, the man entirely vanished before help could be fetched. All of the witnesses report that the man's clothing was very antiquated.

Is it just the local spread of gossip or lore that has led to so many separate reports of the same phenomenon (i.e. "copy-cat" sightings)? The skeptics among us might say so, though it should be noted that all of the various witnesses to the phenomenon were intelligent, credible people who related their accounts sincerely and consistently and who had clearly been deeply affected by their spectral encounters at Perryville Pond.

This strange 1969 haunting has not recurred in recent years, at least not to this researcher's knowledge. Interestingly, a Rehoboth family living in the immediate area claims that one of their relatives—a great uncle who died many years ago—was bitten by a snapping turtle at Perryville Pond in 1889 and was traumatized by the incident for the rest of his life. Was his emotional reaction at the time of the incident so powerful that it is still somehow "impressed" on the place more than a century later?

2) Alleged Incident Date—Ca. early 1970's:

A local surveyor reports that a 150-year-old stone wall, in a wooded area in the central Rehoboth area, was disassembled by workers for the purpose of land clearing and eventual development. Just four days later, the stone wall—some 35 yards of it—was found to be entirely and inexplicably reassembled to its original state (a task that would have required months of skillful labor). The wall was eventually disassembled again by the workers, with no recurrence of the unexplained, phantom reassembly. However, the homeowner who had first hired the workers to take down the wall (to clear the way for his new house) reports that, "Every few months, for the first two years after the house was built, large rocks left over from the wall were (inexplicably) thrown against the side of the house late at night by some (invisible) force."

The odd occurrences eventually ceased, and, at present, the haunting remains inactive. Witnesses to the event speculate that perhaps the disgruntled spirit of some 19th-century farmer, upset that his meticulously-constructed stone wall had been pulled apart by the workers, was responsible for the strange happenings.

3) Alleged Incident Date—Ca. mid-1970's:

Providence resident Janet Russo, while riding with her brother, David, on horse trails situated within the general area of the Palmer River Riding Club in Rehoboth, purportedly encountered a young female Native American, topless and wearing only a breech clout, quickly scurrying off the trail in front of her and her brother as their horses approached. The 48-year-old woman (a medical technician) and her brother immediately stopped their horses and called out to the strange woman, who failed to respond. After resuming their ride down the trail, the perplexed sister and brother soon encountered the Native girl again, who this time manifested herself in such a way as to clearly suggest to the riders that they were witnessing a ghost.

"She floated quickly across the trail in front of us," Janet recalls. "She was kind of angled forward as she floated and her feet were about three feet off the ground...I mean she was really floating mid-air, looking at us with this incredibly (powerful) and angry stare. She also threw a small log at us as she passed across the trail in front of us, but the log vanished in mid-air before it reached us. Then she vanished, too, but not before we saw that she was semi-translucent (unlike her first appearance on the trail, when she had seemed more solid)."

Janet says this was the first and last time she has ever experienced anything supernatural. Her brother, she indicates, was so upset by the ghostly encounter that he refuses to talk about it to the present day (though, in a nervous and cursory manner, he did confirm the incident to this author).

Although Janet and her brother never reported the incident to the Palmer River Riding Club for fear of sounding crazy, at least two other riders in the area claim to have encountered the entity (both sightings purportedly took place circa 1975 and were very similar to Janet's and her brother's experience). Interestingly, although it would only be discernible to the trained eye of an archaeologist and is known only to several local researchers, there is a very small ancient Native American campsite, perhaps 600-900 years old, buried not too far from the general vicinity of the sightings.

ALGONQUIN INDIAN GHOSTS

Introductory Note: I came across the following Algonquin ghost accounts while engaged in research for a forthcoming book on Native American culture in New England. These curious incidents were recorded by several New England Indian groups. These accounts date to the Historic Period (i.e. after the point of colonial contact). To retain the narrative integrity of the following accounts, I repeat them here verbatim as they appear in their original sources, some of which represent the works of 19th and early 20th-century Indian writers.

The Silver Pipe
(Wampanoag, Southeastern Massachusetts-Historic Period)

"King James of England, on hearing the goodness and virtues of Massasoit, once sent him a present of a silver pipe. The Chieftan prized it highly as a gift from his 'white brother over the sea.' But one of his warriors did a deed of valor that so won his heart that he resolved to make him a present of the pipe as his choice treasure. The warrior, finding himself about to die, charged his squaw to put the silver pipe into his grave at the burial, but she, out of regard to the value of the treasure, hid it, and covered the grave without it. One evening she went to the place where she had hidden the royal present, resolving to smoke from the pipe alone, and to hide it again. She put out her hand to take the pipe, but it moved away from her. Again, but it moved away, and again and again...(a) dead hand was moving it. Then she bitterly repented of her disobedience, and promised to bury the pipe if she were able. At this resolution,

the pipe lay still, and she opened the grave, fulfilled the warrior's command, and was enabled to smoke in peace of mind and conscience, we may hope, the rest of her days."

Butterworth, as quoted in Simmons: 124

Peter Sky Changed To A Rock
(Scaticook, Litchfield County, Conn., Historic Period)

"This is the story of Peter Sky...He used to go by a swamp that lay near a road. One dark night he and someone else went to town and got some whiskey. Then they came down that road until they reached the swamp. They took their whiskey down there and began to drink when they had found a nice place to sit on. Soon they fell to quarreling over their whiskey and in the fight that followed Pete was killed. The other Indian got away and was never heard of again. But the next day some people coming by found Pete's body there and a rock with a hole in it close by. That rock was never noticed much by the Indians thereafter until one dark and foggy night, when some of them went down to the swamp on their way home to drink something they had brought. They heard noises from the rock, and one of them poured some of the goods into the hole. Immediately there was a voice from the rock. It called for more, and they kept on pouring whiskey in until the voice was the voice of a drunken man. The rock (which contained the soul of Pete) will 'holler' now on foggy nights if you pour whiskey into it."

Speck, as quoted in Simmons: 125

Tree Ghosts
(Narragansett Tribe, Rhode Island, Historic Period)

"...it is said, that each of the spruce trees (in rural parts of Rhode Island) grows where a drop of Narragansett blood was shed. They will ever grow in South County, no matter how much civilization crowds them. It is said of one settler, that he decided to cut down every spruce tree on his 500 acres of Indian land because they haunted him, and he was killed in the attempt. He cut with such vengeance, when he heard the story that each spruce was the soul of a Narragansett killed by a white man, that a stately spruce which he set out to destroy fell upon him and killed him.

They really do look, as they stand here, there, and everywhere throughout the Narragansett country, that they are souls of departed Red Folk."

Red Wing, as quoted in Simmons: 142

On The Tracks
(Niantic, Bradford, Rhode Island, Historic Period)

" Many years ago a tribe of Niantic Indians lived on the location of the town of Bradford, Rhode Island. In the early part of 1800, the New York, New Haven, and Hartford Line put a railroad from Stonington to Providence. There were a number of the tribe that lived there at that time. The railroad crossed a swamp between Westerly, (R.I.) and Bradford, which was known as White Dog Swamp. Many years ago an Indian and his dog were going home, taking a short cut by the railroad. They were killed by the train. Ever since on dark

73

nights, the dog and the Indian have been seen there. The great white dog will be seen coming down the track cut in two, while the Indian beside him has no head. They go down the middle of the track as far as the brook and then disappear. Many have seen this and the story keeps many away from there on dark nights; but the swamp is still called the White Dog Swamp, to this day."

Lone Wolf, as quoted in Simmons: 140

Woman Afloat
(Wampanoag, Southeastern Massachusetts, Historic Period)

"At a certain spot near the ridge of the cliffs (of Gay Head) an old woman is sometimes seen floating through the air carrying a basket of fish."

Tantaquidgeon, as quoted in Simmons: 139

The Haunted Swamp
(Mohegan, Connecticut, Historic Period)

"(One) time Tantaquidgeon was riding home, and when he was passing the...swamp two dogs dashed from the bushes, and from their mouths they breathed fire. They ran along side, blowing flames at the horse's flanks until he passed the swamp. A white horse's head has been seen lying there too, but when the person approached it, it (moved away). Women who have gone...near the swamp at night have felt hands holding onto their skirts, and even herds of pigs have dashed out to terrify belated travelers at night. Some Indians claim to have felt hands grasping their feet as they went by."

Speck, as quoted in Simmons: 129

74

Good Luck, Or The Ghost That Wasn't
(Narragansett Tribe, Rhode Island, Historic Period)

"How many of us have seen a ghost? I have! About 20 years ago one evening I went fishing some three miles from my home in the woods. About midnight the fog came in from the sea and hid the moon and the stars. I said it is time to go home and after walking about half a mile, I looked up and right beside me was a pillar of fire. As I watched, it turned to green and then to white and went out. I walked on and there it was again; I thought it moved and changed colors. The wind blew and I was about to head for parts unknown, but I seemed glued to the spot. I said the Great Spirit has sent me a sign, so I stood and watched it. Finally, I walked up to where I thought I had seen the ghost and put out my hand. I touched something that was cold, wet and slimy. It felt like something from another world. I backed off and lit a match and there was my ghost. It was an old rotten stump covered with fungus growth; when the damp air settled on it, and the wind blew it, it glowed, changed colors, and faded. Look in the woods for them on a damp night. They are a sign of Good Luck to you."

Red Wing, as quoted in Simmons: 143

Primary Reference: Simmons, William. *Spirit of the New England Tribes.* Princeton: University Press of New England, 1980.

MORE ALGONQUIN GHOST LORE

To the Native American, the dark forest has always been a haunted dwelling place of lurking dead spirits. Mysterious nighttime laughter echoes through the woods...spectral hands rise up from the swamps...faces of long-dead relatives appear in the mist...ancient voices whisper out in the darkness.

Most Algonquin ghost accounts are entertainingly presented as actual occurrences, although, like all cultural folklore, their secondary nature is clearly sociological. From an anthropological standpoint, it is interesting to note that Indian ghost lore became most abundant subsequent to white colonial dissolution of Native culture. Folklorist William Simmons notes that "ghost folklore (was important) functionally. After the (white) contact period, (ghosts) appeared to Indians to warn them against departing from ancestral ways...spirits appeared to the living, urging them to uphold customs and guard socially correct values and behavior."

Our first account reflects a clearly discernible social function. In this instance, the alleged incident serves as a warning against the failure to observe traditional burial customs. The incident in question is said to have occurred at Gay Head:

Haunted Grave
(Wampanoag, Circa 1904, Massachusetts)

"The old folks tell of one good, industrious squaw who died and was buried, and whose sorrowing but

thrifty husband withheld from her grave the pestle she had been accustomed to use. As he had never been known to personally use the article, it was clear that he must have wanted it for some bride-to-be. It so happened that his wife was buried down near the creek and from the surrounding hills a good view could be had of her grave. One evening the 'bereaved' husband was seen to approach the grave and disconsolately cast himself thereon in grief. He made a great display of pretended hypocrisy, but evidently the dead squaw's spirit could not tolerate his hypocrisy and crocodile tears, for the mourning husband was seen to suddenly rise and begin (to frantically run) into the distance. Some say that the dead wife had merely raised herself from her grave and demanded what belonged to her—her pestle. We only know that the husband is running yet."

Our next account similarly affords a cultural warning, this one stressing the consequences of neglecting nuclear-familial values. The following account allegedly explains the unusual reddish discoloration that appears on "Papoose Rock" in Connecticut:

The Bloody Image At Papoose Rock
(Mohegan, Circa 1905, Connecticut)

"A short distance south of Shantic Point is Muddy Cove, the Indian name for which is Basagwanantaksag (derivative from 'basag,' mud). Southwest from this

cove is a rocky ledge on the hillside, at the foot of which is one place where there is a reddish discoloration of the rock, having the general outline of a human figure sprawled out. It is called Papoose Rock and the following tale accounts for this peculiarity:

There was a Mohegan who went across to Long Island and took a wife from one of the tribes there. After some time, he tired of her and came home. Soon after, she had a child. She said to herself, 'My child's father has left me to take care of him. I cannot do it alone.' So she made ready for a journey and set out for the Mohegan country across the Sound to look for her husband. She found him at Mohegan and said to him, 'You must take care of me and the child.' But he paid no attention to her. Then she went down to where there was a steep sloping rock not far from the river. Standing at the top of this slope, she took her child in one hand and grasped its head with the other. Then she twisted the head and it came off, the blood flowing down the rocks. The woman cast the head down, and the body she threw farther out. Where the head fell there remained a splotch of blood, and where the body struck there was left an imprint stained upon the rock in the shape of the child. The (red markings) are still there, and (they) tell of her deed."

Not all Algonquin ghost accounts, however, so readily address sociological issues. Some, in fact, seem simply intended to frighten and entertain. The following three accounts, all of which are allegedly true, are textured examples. In all three incidents, the ghostly manifestations involve strange lights and illuminations, a phenomenon quite common in New England Algonquin ghost lore:

Glowing Spirit
(Mohegan Tribe, Circa 1909, Connecticut)

"One dark, stormy night a woman was coming down a long hill toward Two Bridges, having been up to New London. Looking across the swamp to the opposite slope she beheld a light approaching in her direction. When they drew near to one another the woman saw that the light was suspended in the center of a person's stomach as though in a frame. There was no shadow cast, and yet the outline of the person could be distinguished as it surrounded the light. The woman was badly frightened and ran all the way home."

Old Peckham House
(Narraganset Tribe, Circa 1984, Rhode Island)

"This happened recently. My daughter and another kid went to the old abandoned Peckham house, past Signal Rock near Church Road. They went there junking. It was light. They were looking for copper, brass, lead,—things to sell. They were in the place

and it started to get dark. They had flashlights with them. They drove out and one wanted to go back and look in a shed. They looked back and there was a light in the upstairs window. One said, 'Did you leave a flashlight?' The other said no. It looked like a yellow lantern light. They went back and went through the whole house, and nothing. No sign of a lantern or anything else. And the sun had been set for over an hour and a half. They began to leave and then they saw the light in the upstairs window again. They knew that the light shouldn't be there."

Ghostly Lights
(Mohegan Tribe, Circa, 1905, Connecticut)

"Mrs. Fielding (an Indian) was aroused one night by a light that shone from the hill above her house, and while she stood watching it from the window, she saw it ascend the hill to a small heap of rocks, where it blazed up high and subsided. Then it moved to another rock and blazed up high again, subsiding as before in a few moments. She had reason to be certain that no one was in the pasture, and the next morning she found no evidence of burning about the rocks. The thing was repeated a number of times and she considered herself to have been visited by spirits."

Our last account is perhaps the strangest. While not a generalized tribal account, it does derive from a Native American and contains some typical elements of Algonquin ghost lore (most notably, mysterious manifestations of light and an affirmation of life after death). The incident in question allegedly took place on Cape Cod many years ago. It was related to me by an elderly Native American woman in the summer of 1993:

The Luminescent Soul
(Wampanoag, Modern Period, Cape Cod)

"I was just a girl at the time. It was late evening, and I was walking alone on the beach. The moon was full (so) I could see my way. All of a sudden, I noticed a bluish light underneath the waves. The light was moving under the water just a few yards off shore. I stopped and watched it. I was (curious) and I walked closer to it, toward the edge of the water. By now the light was glowing very bright blue. It was round, about the size of a (basketball), and it was still moving around under the water. I began to feel afraid. I knew it wasn't the reflection of the moon. Suddenly, the ball of light rose up from the water and (hovered) in the air a few yards in front of me. I just froze, and the light floated there for maybe a minute. It seemed peaceful and warm. Then, the ball of light shot down the beach. It shot off so fast it was like a bullet. Within a matter of seconds it disappeared into the distance. I went home, feeling very shaken up. I lived about a quarter-mile from the beach.

The next afternoon, I heard my family talking about a drowning. A young woman had drowned while swimming in the ocean the night before. They said where it happened, and I realized (it was) the exact spot on the beach where I saw the strange bright light rise up from the water. And I learned the drowning had taken place about the same time I was on the beach. I never actually saw the drowning girl, but I had seen her spirit or soul taking flight. That was the beautiful ball of light. I have never been afraid of dying since then."

What had this woman actually seen at the beach? Was the mysterious "ball of light" just a reflection of the full moon on the water, later embellished by the woman's imagination when she learned of the drowning? Probably. But whether real or imagined, this woman's experience affected her strongly.

A REHOBOTH POLTERGEIST

When it comes to ghosts, there is probably no one who takes them more seriously than Hans Holzer. Professor Holzer, who holds a Ph.D. and who has authored some 70 books and articles dealing with supernatural phenomena, is perhaps America's foremost researcher in the field of parapsychology. As a professional "ghost hunter," Holzer has traveled to just about every state in the country, hot on the trail of the restless spirits and disembodied souls that make things go bump in the night. He has braved the dusty attics and dark cellars of old homes whose owners report horrific hauntings and bizarre goings-on. In his tireless research, the professor has sought to record and document these strange occurrences and, where possible, to communicate with the ghosts responsible for them.

Of course, there are some skeptics who say that Dr. Holzer, despite his respectable credentials, is someone who suffers from an acutely hyperactive imagination. Be that as it may, the cases he has documented make for wonderful reading in front of the fireplace on a stormy night. Fact or fiction, his ghostly accounts send tingles up the spine. One of Holzer's best-documented hauntings is described by the researcher in his book *Yankee Ghosts* (Dublin, N.H.: Yankee Books, 1966). In May of 1964, writes the professor, he was contacted by one Doris Armfield of Rehoboth, Massachusetts, who complained of poltergeist activity in her 200 year-old Rehoboth home. Mrs. Armfield described the first unearthly occurrences as follows:

> *My husband and I were eating supper, when a sound like an explosion made us both bound from our chairs. We found that a glass dish in the kitchen cupboard on the top shelf had shattered.*

At first, Mr. and Mrs. Armfield concluded that a fluctuation in room temperature had caused the spontaneous breakage of glass. Over the next few years, however, additional occurrences of a strange and inexplicable nature would convince the Armfields that they were sharing their Rehoboth home with one or more restless phantoms.

Two years after the mysterious shattering of the glass dish, Mrs. Armfield began to sense the presence of some dark and other-worldly entity within her house. In her description to professor Holzer, she states that:

> *My husband joined the Navy, and his aunt came to stay with me. The first night as we sat down to supper in the kitchen, my dog, Dusty, sat beside my chair, and all of a sudden he started to growl very deeply. The hackles rose on his back, he bared his teeth, and scared me half to death, because I had never seen him do this unless he thought I was threatened. He was staring at an empty chair to my left...but no one was there.*

The dog and Mrs. Armfield strongly sensed that some invisible and sinister presence was sitting in that chair. The following week, according to Mrs. Armfield's account, the unearthly happenings in her home became even more disturbing.

Repeatedly, the woman would hear the sound of smashing glass, only to find that nothing in the house had broken:

> *My husband's aunt went home, and I was alone. One night I was reading in bed, with the dog at my feet. I reached up to put off the bed lamp when I heard a tremendous crash and the sound of dishes banging, crashing, and shattering. I guessed immediately that the dish cupboard in the kitchen had fallen loose from the wall and had spewed the hundreds of dishes across the floor and smashed them to smithereens. But I flew into the kitchen only to find that everything was intact. I took a flashlight and went all over the house from cellar to attic...nothing was broken.*

Over the ensuing months, Mrs. Armfield would frequently hear the same "horrible clashing and clattering of dishes being broken," only to again find that not a single dish in the house had actually been damaged. When her husband was home, he heard the same phantom noises, as did many other visitors to the house. In her description to Professor Holzer, Mrs. Armfield reports that:

> *A neighbor and myself were singing, and also playing the piano in the dining room, and we were tape recording our efforts. At the end of the song, we heard a crash of dishes or glasses, and we ran to the kitchen. Once again, nothing was broken. I then thought of the fact that the crash might be on the tape, and we played it back and sure enough, we heard it loud and clear.*

85

The tape, if genuine, was the most objective piece of evidence for an actual haunting within the Armfields' Rehoboth home. What was the meaning of these unnatural, ghostly noises? What malevolent presence had so unsettled the Armfields' dog? Was some spectral entity trying to frighten the Armfields out of the house? Did the home's 200 year history contain some dark and twisted secret?

These questions many never be answered. Though Professor Holzer felt that Mrs. Armfield's account was credible, the woman died before the professor had an opportunity to visit the house to further investigate. Says Holzer in his book: "after the wife had passed away, I decided, under the circumstances, not to trouble the husband. Mrs. Armfield herself might have discovered what or who it was that caused the uncanny noises in the Rehoboth house—from her side of the veil."

TERROR IN THE TREETOPS

*Introductory Note: In order to include an important haunting from the northern part of the region, the following allegedly true account is excerpted—for those who have not yet read it— from the author's best-selling and critically-acclaimed collection of true ghost accounts, **The New England Ghost Files** (Covered Bridge Press—1994).*

Dick and Marjorie Dennet, who live in Vermont's lovely Green Mountains, have experienced a unique type of haunting. They do not have a haunted house; what they did have on their property was a haunted tree—an old oak tree which allegedly exuded a very dark and frightening energy.

"Some very strange things have happened in the immediate area of the tree," says Marjorie, "and I eventually stopped going near it. Fortunately, it was on the far end of the property, opposite the pastures and far away from the house, so it was easy for me to avoid it. Still, in time, things got so frightening with that tree that we had to cut it down."

Dick adds: "The first disturbing occurrences took place about twenty years ago, when we first bought the farm. One morning, we found both of our cats dead, and they were lying right by that old oak tree. There were no signs of visible injuries, and we had the cats autopsied by our veterinarian. He found absolutely nothing wrong with them, and he was at a complete loss to explain how they had died. On other occasions, we found dead birds around the same tree—and that tree only. It was very (perplexing)."

"One time," adds Marjorie, "I was taking a walk across the property with my dog, Jasper. As we approached the oak tree, Jasper began to growl at it. Then he just dashed off—which is totally unlike him—as if he wanted to get away from that tree as quickly as possible. Many times after that, if I led Jasper anywhere near the tree, he would become extremely agitated and would growl at it. It was incredible the way the tree affected him. Finally, one afternoon about four months later, I found him lying motionless by the tree. He was dead, like the cats."

Dick and Marjorie indicated that their daughter also had a bizarre experience while playing near the tree many years ago.

"She was six or seven at the time, and she came running to the house crying," Dick remembers. "We asked her what had happened, and she said that she had heard a disembodied voice by the tree. She said that the voice sounded like a young boy's—that at first it was a friendly and gentle voice...telling her she was pretty and other nice things. But after a while, she said, the voice inexplicably changed. It began to get louder and angrier, yelling and cursing at her. This was very hard for us to believe at the time, but it was obvious that something had frightened her terribly. She never played near the tree again."

"And it became even more ominous," added Marjorie. "My father visited us in early 1973, and he had a heart attack while taking a walk on the property. Fortunately, he survived, but I find it strange that his heart attack took place right by that old oak tree. I think that something frightened him horribly there, but, to this day, he won't talk about it. He gets very tense and edgy whenever I ask him about what happened that day; he doesn't reply and just leaves the room."

Dick indicates that the strangest occurrence of all took place in July of 1973.

"I had just mowed the pastures," he recalls, "and I was riding past the old oak tree on my tractor. I suddenly noticed that there was a young boy, maybe sixteen or seventeen, sitting up in one of the branches, staring down at me. I stopped the tractor next to the tree and called up to the boy to ask him who he was and what he was doing there. He responded by spitting at me and using all sorts of foul language. He looked strange—very thin and pale. I told him to get off my property or I would call the police, but he just began to laugh. I got back on the tractor and started back toward the house. As I began to drive away, I glanced back at the tree for one more look at this strange youngster. When I did, though, I was shocked to see that he was no longer there in the tree. He had simply vanished."

Five months later, at which point they were already contemplating cutting down the oak tree even though it was one of very few oaks on their property, Marjorie and Dick received a startling bit of information.

"The town tax assessor came out to the farm to reevaluate the property," says Marjorie. "He's an old-timer in town, and he knows a lot about the town's history. When he came out to the farm, he asked us in passing if we knew about Joshua. We told him we had no idea what he was talking about. He then proceeded to tell us about a boy named Joshua—the son of one of the farm's previous owners—who killed himself on the property in 1943. When we asked him how he did it, the tax assessor pointed in the direction of the old oak tree and said that the boy had hanged himself from one of the tree's branches. Needless to say, this information was extremely disturbing to us. This was the same tree where all the weird things had been happening. I guess it was then that we first began to wonder if the tree had a ghost."

"When I heard that," adds Dick, "I immediately cut the tree down. I didn't know if it would help or not, but I should have done it a lot sooner. It was obvious that there was something very wrong with that tree, and, as crazy as it sounds, I believe that the boy I saw up in the branches was the ghost of Joshua."

Marjorie thinks that she now may understand the haunting:

"Considering all that happened around that tree, it is our belief that Joshua's suicide—and we have no idea what caused it—remained unresolved. All of his anger, pain, and guilt were somehow still present at the scene of his death—attached to that oak tree because that's where he hung himself. Somehow, when that tree was removed, the spirit—at least we think—chose to move out of the area. Maybe that's because the tree was no longer there to remind him of his suicide. It seems silly, we realize, but the strange occurrences completely stopped after Dick cut down the tree. Still, we mostly avoid the spot where that old tree used to stand...just in case."

Author's Note: Research reveals that a suicide by hanging—involving a teenage boy—did occur on the property in December of 1943.

CHAPTER THREE

AMAZING YANKEES

THE ASTONISHING
WOMEN OF SOUTHERN NEW ENGLAND

The history of southern New England is rife with accounts of colorful women whose incredibly unusual lives were far ahead of their times. For instance, during the 1780's, Deborah Gannett of Sharon, Massachusetts, joined the Continental Army and fought honorably in several military skirmishes—successfully avoiding detection by disguising herself as a man! This woman, and several others whose lives are equally striking, will be the focus of this section.

Too often, early commentators afford scant attention to the women who defied the historical contexts in which they lived—women whose refreshingly liberal spirits forged their own equality at a time when society was not yet ready to concede it.

Deborah Sampson Gannett

In 1782, a rugged 22 year-old lad named Robert Shurtleff showed up in Worcester to enlist in the Continental Army. He was passed for enlistment and marched with 50 other young recruits to West Point—where he was issued a uniform, a gun, and field gear. If, at this point in history, there had been physical exams for enlisting soldiers, the examiner may have found that Robert Shurtleff was missing that one crucial thing that all other soldiers had. Robert Shurtleff was, in fact, one Deborah Sampson Gannett of Massachusetts, a young woman who was determined to serve her struggling country on the battlefield.

Robert, a.k.a. Deborah, participated in several military skirmishes. During a military encounter in Tarrytown, New York, she was shot in the leg and dressed her own wounds. Several months later, while involved in another encounter at Philadelphia, Deborah contracted typhoid fever. This time, there was no avoiding an exam by military physicians, who quickly discovered that Robert was certainly not a Robert. The army reacted by discharging Deborah in 1783, but, notably, the discharge was an honorable one. Deborah soon married and had three children. Although Deborah was initially denied a usual soldier's pension, Paul Revere, several years later, succeeded not only in securing a small army pension for her, but also back pay. When Deborah died in 1827, her husband, Benjamin Gannett, requested a widower's pension from the government. It was the first time in American history that a man sought a widower's pension for his wife's military service. The Congress not only granted the pension, but also acknowledged Deborah as a fully legitimate soldier and war hero. In the summer of 1983, the state House of Representatives declared Deborah Gannett the Official Heroine of the Commonwealth.

Lydia Pinkham

Although not as well known today, Lydia Pinkham's name was a household word during the later part of the 19th-century. In 1857, after the death of her husband, this innovative New Englander founded the Lydia E. Pinkham Medicine Company at the age of 57. At a time when few women dared or were allowed to enter the business world, Lydia built a thriving enterprise in the kitchen of her Lynn, Massachusetts, home—

an enterprise that would quickly grow into a $4 million dollar business with an annual gross of $300,000.

Lydia's Vegetable Compound for Female Complaints became world renowned, and she eventually marketed her women's cure-all in 33 different countries. Her medicine contained unicorn root, black cohosh, and pleursy root. Being the astute business woman that she was, Lydia also added another key ingredient that was sure to give a little "kick" both to her medicine and to her annual sales. Despite the fact that Lydia was a strong advocate of the temperance movement, her medicinal contained 18% alcohol. Perhaps part of the medicine's success was due to the fact that it made it easy for women to imbibe at a time when such a past-time was reserved mostly for men.

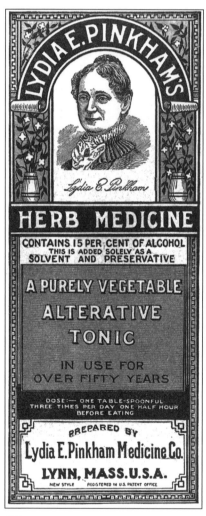

Lydia's most brilliant business move was to place her picture on every bottle of medicine she sold. Her reassuring, sweet, and maternal face brought comfort to ailing women (and money to Lydia's coffers). Lydia's became the best known female face in America during the later part of the 19th-century.

Unfortunately, Lydia's medicine was not potent enough to cure her own illness in 1883. After her death, her children took over the thriving business, and it remained a family operation until 1973. At that time, the business was still grossing about $700,000 dollars annually.

Ida Lewis

If you were a sailor during the later part of the 19th-century, and your ship happened to be sinking off the coast of Newport, Rhode Island, it wouldn't have been the Coast Guard that came to your rescue. Rather, a gusty woman named Ida Lewis would have been the first person to reach you with a life boat, and, whatever your catastrophe, she would have calmly negotiated you out of it.

Ida Lewis, born in 1842, was the keeper of the Newport lighthouse at Lime Rock for over fifty years. During that time, she braved the cold waters of Newport Harbor to save drowning swimmers, boaters, and even animals (she once saved a sheep that had fallen off a barge belonging to Newport millionaire August Belmont).

For her many acts of bravery, Ida was the recipient of numerous awards and tributes, including the first gold lifesaving medal ever issued by the U. S. government.

Ida died in 1911, taking with her many local sailors' peace of mind.

Maria Mitchell

Maria Mitchell, one of Nantucket's famous daughters, was born on the island in 1818. Despite the small, limited world of island life, Maria's keen mind and intellect soared to the heavens: literally.

Maria established an observatory at her home and became America's first female astronomer. She earned an international reputation when she discovered a new comet in 1847, an accomplishment which earned her a gold medal from the king of Denmark. The following year, she became the first woman fellow of the American Academy of Arts and Sciences. In 1861, at a time when few women ever attended college, Maria began to teach it. She was appointed professor of astronomy at Vassar College and served as the director of its observatory until her death in 1880.

Maria's home and observatory are now part of the Maria Mitchell Association on Nantucket. The attraction now also includes a science library, a museum of natural science, and an aquarium.

Lucy Stone

Lucy Stone, of Brookfield, Massachusetts, was a member of one of New England's foremost families. In 1847, at a time when college educations were reserved almost exclusively for men, Lucy surprised everyone by announcing that she would enroll at Oberlin College. Not only did she enroll, but she graduated with high honors, and she was requested to write the college's commencement address.

Lucy refused the request. Her reason: at this time in history, public speeches and lectures by women were generally forbidden. Lucy had no intentions of writing a commencement address unless she, herself, could give it.

In 1855, Lucy married Henry Blackwell, himself a liberal and a staunch opponent of slavery. In a show of independence virtually unheard of at that time, Lucy not only drew up her own marriage contract, but also retained her maiden name.

Lucy went on to become a pioneering figure in the early struggle for women's rights. At a time when few women spoke out in public, she became a popular lecturer on issues of gender equality. She also founded a highly esteemed publication that was known in its day as "the voice of the women's movement."

As she lay dying of a stomach tumor on October 18, 1893, Lucy whispered to her daughter, Alice, "Make the world a better place." Even in death, this independent spirit refused to relinquish control of her own destiny. She left detailed funeral instructions that were carried out to the letter, including instructions for the cremation of her body. Hers was the first cremation ever recorded in Massachusetts. In death, as in life, Lucy refused to follow the norm.

THE AMAZING STORY OF DALLAS BOUSHEY

As a student of New England history, I find myself especially attracted to historical figures who, while quite extraordinary in their attainments, have never made it into the mainstream history books. When perusing old newspapers and documents, I am astounded by the number of strikingly colorful and unusually accomplished characters, both men and women, of whom little or nothing has ever been recorded. Indeed, as one of my archaeological colleagues often says to me, "Our history books don't have a clue."

Following is an account of an obscure but astounding New England character. While he doesn't appear in any mainstream history books, he certainly belongs there.

Dallas Boushey

Dallas Boushey, a native of South Burlington, Vermont, began work at the University of Vermont College of Medicine in the late 1930's. In time, he eventually became one of the school's most distinguished professors of anatomy. While these facts in themselves are not so remarkable, they become so when we consider that Professor Boushey was an eighth-grade drop-out who was hired by the college as a janitor! Without taking so much as a single formal anatomy course, the self-taught Boushey eventually worked his way into a fully tenured medical school professorship, and he did so without so much as a high school diploma.

In 1937, when he began work at the medical school sweeping and mopping floors, Boushey immediately impressed the staff with his diligence and reliability. Of course, none of the anatomy professors imagined that the efficient janitor would someday become one of their most respected colleagues. At that time, Boushey didn't even know what the word "anatomy" meant. He seemed fully content as an ordinary maintenance man, and, without even a high school degree, how far could he expect to advance at a prestigious medical school?

In 1940, Boushey's exceptional job performance caught the attention of anatomy professor Dr. Walter Stultz. Stultz asked Boushey to take charge of laboratory maintenance. In addition to sweeping, mopping, and keeping the laboratories thoroughly spotless, Boushey's new duties also included assisting Dr. Stultz with the embalming of corpses.

Dr. Stultz was startled by how quickly the janitor mastered all of the embalming procedures. Realizing that Boushey's apparent intelligence could be put to better use, the physician taught Boushey how to assist with dissections. Before long, Boushey had helped Dr. Stultz to develop a method for retrieving delicate human bones with which the medical students could study. Boushey, now involved in something far more sophisticated than simple sweeping and mopping, became fascinated by the new work, but he also felt frustrated by his thorough lack of knowledge.

He began to ask questions. "What are the names of those muscles and bones? How do they function? How are they attached?" As Dr. Stultz recalled many years later, the bright janitor "wanted to know it all. I taught him the information as we worked. He would remember the names and repeat them to me the next day. It was at this point that I realized Dallas Boushey was unique. Even with his lack of education, he had the innate intelligence to learn the material."

One evening, Boushey asked Dr. Stultz if he could borrow a copy of *Gray's Anatomy*. With its complex terminology and diagrams, the book was very difficult reading for a man with an eighth-grade education. At first it seemed impossible to Dr. Stultz that Boushey could ever grasp all of the material. But the eager janitor had made up his mind. Every evening after dinner, Boushey wrestled with the text and delved further and further into the enormous volume, using English and medical dictionaries to look up every word that stumped him. His wife copied passages out of the book and quizzed him on the material. And each morning at work, Boushey would discuss what he had learned with Dr. Stultz.

The faculty of the medical school was startled. One anatomy professor recalled that "Boushey would look up eponyms (uncommonly used names for parts of the body) in the dictionary. He used to bandy these names about and try to mystify the faculty. In time, whenever faculty members had a question about anatomy, they would go and ask the janitor!"

Indeed, after two years of studying the book and performing dissections with Dr. Stultz, Boushey had acquired a knowledge of anatomy that surpassed that of most physicians. Soon, while the students were studying at the anatomy tables during class, Boushey was allowed to go around and answer their questions.

Surprisingly, the medical students did not resent being taught by a high school drop-out. As one student recalled, "Boushey didn't have all that educational mush behind him. He could talk to us in simpler, more understandable terms." Over the next few years, the janitor-turned-scholar became increasingly active in teaching. And although he didn't have so much as a high school diploma, he became a favored faculty member among the students. "He was more on our level than the other professors were," recalled one student. "He was gentle and down-to-earth. We could really talk to him."

Even greater achievements were soon to come. In 1944, when his students complained about the confusing nature of the one-dimensional illustrations in their anatomy books, it occurred to Boushey that anatomy would be easier for the students to comprehend if they could actually pick up and closely examine three-dimensional models. Boushey coiled stovepipe wires, wrapped them in gauze, and painted them in latex. In time, he had constructed sophisticated models of virtually every part of the human body. Over the next twenty years, his models were displayed and utilized at medical schools throughout the country. Across the nation, professors had a difficult time believing that these highly technical and anatomically precise models were the work of a high school drop-out and former janitor. Still, there was no disputing that the models were the most sophisticated and advanced of their kind.

By the 1960's, Boushey was teaching anatomy at the medical college full-time, and there were more and more inquiries as to his official status. School administrators began scratching their heads. How could they formally classify a brilliant teacher who, although he had risen to become the college's most popular and knowledgeable teacher of anatomy, had begun work as a janitor and held not even a basic high school diploma? The administrators tried out several new titles on Boushey, including "senior technician" and "demonstrator in anatomy." But somehow, considering that Boushey was the school's foremost expert in human anatomy, the titles seemed inadequate. Still, as Boushey was an eighth-grade drop-out, he could not legally be referred to as "Doctor" Boushey.

Finally, in 1972, Dr. William Young, then chairman of the anatomy department, suggested that the University of Vermont Board of Trustees afford Boushey a full professorship in anatomy. In other words, without having even graduated high school, Boushey would henceforth be known as "Professor Boushey" and would enjoy a salary and tenure appropriate for the position. The Board of Trustees pondered the recommendation and finally, when student and faculty voted Boushey Teacher of the Year for 1972, granted the former janitor a full academic professorship.

Despite his lofty new position, Boushey did little in the way of altering his lifestyle to fit his new rank. As his wife put it, "He is one of the most unchangeable people you can imagine. He builds his models, teaches classes, and never stops reading anatomy. He feels uncomfortable at fancy parties. I've even seen him turn red when someone calls him professor. He's still the quiet, modest man he was in 1937." Boushey himself once noted, "These days students ask me whether they should call me doctor or professor. I tell them, 'just call me Dallas'."

By the time he retired, the highly admired professor had made medical history. He was, and remains, the only high school drop-out to become a full professor at a 20th-century medical school, proving that curiosity, experience, and self-motivation, even more than formal degrees and titles, are the precursors of true wisdom.

ASCENT OF A WOMAN

Note: The following article by Mr. Robinson on Annie Smith Peck first appeared in the March, 1997, issue of **Yankee.**

In 1908, a mountaineer from Rhode Island stood proudly at the summit of Mount Huascaran in Peru. The climber had reached some 22,204 feet—1,500 feet higher than Mount McKinley and, at the time, the highest ascent ever made by an American. To the public, the climb itself was less astonishing than the person who made it. Beneath all of the climbing gear—knicker bockers, tunic, stout boots, and woolen hose—was a fifty-eight year-old woman.

Born into an austere, traditional Baptist family in 1850, Annie Smith Peck seemed destined for a quiet life of Victorian conventionality. Her aristocratic mother, a direct descendent of Rhode Island founder Roger Williams, saw to it that Annie was imbued with the manners appropriate for a refined young lady of high social standing. Annie's father, a prominent Rhode Island attorney and businessman, enrolled her in Dr. Stockbridge's School for Young Ladies in Providence. At this time in history her sex precluded college, but Annie was afforded the kind of a classical, properly-constrained "female" education that might someday draw her a socially endowed husband.

It was much to her parents shock, then, when 24-year-old Annie, in 1874, took it upon herself to enroll at the University of Michigan—one of the few colleges in the country that educated women on an equal basis with men. And while the frantic Pecks discussed how they might lure their daughter back into a more conventional life of socially advantageous marriage, Annie went on to secure her B.A. in Greek in 1878, earning honors in all of her courses.

It was now apparent that there would be no steering Annie into timely marriage and motherhood. And soon, Annie would go from shocking her parents to provoking the entire world. While passing through Germany on her way to graduate school in Athens, Annie encountered her first large mountain range. While gazing in awe at the towering "frowning walls" of Germany's Matterhorn, Annie suddenly recalled the powerful frustration she had felt as a girl—an anger that had repeatedly welled up inside her whenever her three brothers, declaring that athletics were beyond her feminine abilities, refused to let her join them in sports.

Back then, Annie had made a vow to herself: someday, she would prove to the male members of her family that she could develop the physical stamina and endurance necessary for athletic performance. And not just performance, but excellence. Now, many years later, she had stumbled across the ideal stage upon which to make her point. Staring excitedly at Germany's sky-scraping Matterhorn, Annie decided that she would soon be climbing mountains.

Though she scaled a couple of small peaks while in Europe, Annie's first important climb did not take place until 1888, after she had returned to America and had begun to establish herself as a lecturer on Greek and Roman archaeology. She ascended Mount Shasta in California (14,162 feet), outraging her parents and all but one of her brothers. While the Pecks thought it horrid that any woman, especially one who was thirty-nine, would display such immodesty, it was socially unbearable that the female in question was a member of their family. Their displeasure, however, served only to goad Annie on. Six years later, in 1895, Annie returned to the formidable Matterhorn range in Germany and ascended its peak at age forty-five, becoming instantly famous and even more notorious.

Annie was slight and feminine—not the Amazon that people expected in a female mountain climber. As daring as she had been to scale the Matterhorn, no one expected that Annie had the strength or endurance to reach the world's most formidable peaks—summits that challenged even the most seasoned male climbers. But soon, as if eager to fly in the face of public disapproval, Annie made her climbs more ambitious. In 1897, she scaled Mexico's Mount Orizaba (18,696 feet), the highest summit in the Americas ever reached by a woman. Annie further provoked the public with her daring and eccentric climbing outfit, which by now had become her trademark. It consisted of hip-length tunic, knickerbockers, stout boots and woolen hose. Topping it all off was a soft felt hat with a veil.

Annie's notoriety began to mix with a certain amount of public popularity. Her lecturing career thrived. By 1900, under professional management, she was giving public talks across the country. Though Annie had become a respected lecturer on archaeology, most people now attended her lectures not to learn about the past but rather to see the slight, delicate Rhode

Islander who had been reaching distances almost 20,000 feet higher than herself. To her financial advantage, Annie began to focus her lectures on her mountaineering exploits.

While attending a mountaineering conference in Europe in 1900, Annie successfully ascended Monte Cristallo in the Dolomites, among others. Still, she had yet to reach a height where, in her own words, "no man had previously stood." Over the next few years, Annie, not discouraged by the fact that she was now in her fifties, searched for that height. Finally, in 1906, she decided on Mount Huascaran in Peru. At a then-estimated height of 25,000 feet, Huascaran, a mountain never before attempted by anyone, seemed to Annie her best chance for a world record.

After two failed attempts in 1906, Annie, with two expert Swiss guides, successfully reached the north summit of Mount Huascaran in 1908. She was somewhat discouraged when one of her over-eager guides hastily stepped onto the summit a few moments before her, but she had succeeded nonetheless. Eventually, it was proven by triangulation that Huascaran was not 25,000 feet but 22,204, meaning that Annie had come close to but had not broken the world record. Still, by reaching the summit of Huascaran, she had climbed higher in the Western Hemisphere than any other American, male or female, had ever ascended. She received a gold medal from the Peruvian Government, and the north peak of Huascaran was eventually named Cumbre Aña Peck in her honor. International acclaim for Annie was now adulatory instead of controversial.

Except for her brother George, no one in Annie's family ever came to terms with her unusual pursuits. Annie never returned home. Nor did she ever marry. She continued to travel and lecture, also publishing articles and books about her climbing adventures. In 1911, at the age of sixty-one, she was the first person to climb the formidable Mount Coropuna (21,079 feet) in Peru. An active member of the woman's suffragist movement, Annie planted a banner—reading "Votes for Women"—at the mountain's summit.

During the late 1920's and early 30's, Annie traveled the entire southern continent promoting commercial aviation. She finally returned to New England in 1932 and climbed her last mountain, New Hampshire's Mount Madison, at the age of eighty-two. When she died in New York three years later, her cremated remains were returned to Rhode Island for burial. Set on Annie's gravestone was an inscription summing up her remarkable life: "You have brought uncommon glory to women of all time."

THE HUNGRY HERO

Note: The following article by Mr. Robinson first appeared in
Yankee.

On the morning of October 23, 1894, Louis Bouchard enjoyed
some good fortune. As the Fall River, Massachusetts, egg
merchant drove his cart along his route, he noticed a wrapped
bundle lying on top of the trolley tracks at the "Westport Four
Corners" intersection. A subscriber to the finders-keepers school
of philosophy, Louis concluded that an unattended package was
his, and he descended from his cart to make the retrieval.

He climbed back in with the bundle under his arm, settled into
his seat, and slowly unwrapped his prize. Louis was delighted
to find that the take was bountiful: four large, plump sausages,
a ready-made breakfast for a hungry man who was sick of
eating eggs. Unable to read English, Louis could not make out
what was written on the large stamps prominently displayed on
each end of the four tubes.

The lucky merchant dug into the end of one of his trophies and
took a taste. He noticed that the flavor was different from that
of any sausage that he ever tasted—and unusually sweet. He
wondered if it was not a sausage at all, but some type of dried
fruit. But he liked the sweet flavor, and after sampling some
more, he decided to find out just what it was.

Louis pulled his cart up to Barre's Drug Store, hoping that
Homer Barre might be able to identify the mysterious stuff. He

proudly unwrapped his find and asked what type of fruit he had been eating. After reading the stamp on one of the tubes, Homer gave Louis a sympathetic look and explained that he had been eating dynamite and was likely, at any moment, to explode.

Horrified, Louis sank helplessly into a chair while Homer fetched help. Officer Louis Moreau soon arrived on the scene, relieved to find that the egg merchant was, at least for the moment, still intact. An explosives expert was summoned, and he identified the "sausages" as high-intensity dynamite. Whoever had placed the dynamite on the tracks had probably meant to blow up the streetcar. If the wheels of a loaded trolley had struck the package, human losses would surely have been staggering.

Fall River's trolley, circa 1894.

112

Thus, what could have been one of the worst disasters in Fall River history was averted—or rather, ingested—by an egg merchant. And what of poor Louis? An article appearing in that day's *Fall River Daily Herald* said that "when restoratives had been applied to Bouchard, he departed aimlessly and is probably treading his way back home with panther-like steps that no sudden jar might set off the explosive he had chewed off the 'sausage'."

There is no report on whether the police ever caught the dynamiters. And Louis, it seems, never did explode.

THE MAN WHO WAS STOOD UP BY GOD

Between March 21, 1843 and March 21, 1844, the world was on the brink of total destruction. Or so a lot of people thought. Many New Englanders destroyed their homes, threw away their money and valuables, and, in some cases, killed their entire families, all because they thought that God's awesome judgment was imminent, and that the planet was about to be destroyed in fiery cataclysm.

The man responsible for this chaotic state of affairs was one William Miller, an atheist-turned-minister from Massachusetts. "Using the periods referred to as 2,300 days, the 'seven times seven' Gentile supremacy, and the 1,335 days in the book of Daniel as prophetic periods, he concluded that Judgment Day would occur between March 21, 1843, and March 21, 1844." *(Those Eccentric Yankees, Camden, Maine: Yankee Books, 1991, 112.)* In 1831, in Dresden, Miller warned a church congregation that four signs would precede the fulfillment of his apocalyptic prophecy:

> 1) Curiosities and wonders would be observed in the sky.
> 2) There would be earthquakes in various parts of the world.
> 3) The planet would be plagued by wars.
> 4) Mankind would exhibit marked intelligence and advancement.

Not long after, much to the astonishment of his listeners, the four "signs" became manifest.

1) On November 1, 1833, a blazing meteor shower illuminated the sky for fifty minutes.

2) There were reports of earthquakes in England, the West Indies, India, and elsewhere.

3) Revolutions began to occur in various parts of Europe.

4) Numerous technological inventions and advancements appeared in the wake of industrialization.

Miller's prophetic message spread like wildfire, and the self-styled Massachusetts minister soon found himself with thousands of followers (who came to be known as "Millerites"). In speeches delivered throughout the east, Miller convinced more and more people that the world would, in fact, come to an end between March 21, 1843, and March 21, 1844. Throughout New England and other parts of eastern America, Millerites held mass demonstrations at which they prayed, sang, and sobbed in anticipation of God's awesome destruction of the planet.

As the fateful time grew closer, Miller's followers, convinced that they were soon to be swept up into Heaven, began to behave more and more erratically. In January of 1843, when unusual solar phenomena appeared in the sky over New York City, many Millerites destroyed their homes and property and proceeded to establish Millerite "camps," where they set up tents, sang, prayed and awaited the awesome end of the world.

Some Millerites killed their families and themselves, believing that the dead would be the first to enjoy resurrection into Heaven. Many betrothed girls, to the great frustration of their new husbands, would not allow their marriages to be consummated, preferring instead to enter Heaven as virgins. One Millerite woman from Windsor, Connecticut, believing that God had infused her with miraculous powers, attempted to take a stroll across a river. Finding herself unable to walk on water, however, she quickly sank to her demise. Another enthusiastic Millerite, suddenly believing that the Lord had bestowed upon him the ability to fly, drove his horse and buggy over a cliff. Not until he was airborne did he realize that he had perhaps miscalculated his abilities, but by then it was too late for him to counteract the unpleasant effects of gravity.

When the Great Comet of 1843 made its dramatic appearance in the sky, it was a blazing and awesome display; the number of converts flocking into Millerite camps more than doubled. Following this fiery spectacle, Miller revealed to the world its specific day of destruction. The minister stated in the *New York Herald* that God would consume the planet by fire on April 3, 1843. When the fateful day arrived, thousands of Millerites assembled at various cemeteries and hilltops throughout New England and other parts of the east. Donning flowing white robes, they gathered around blazing bonfires, sobbing and prostrating themselves, convinced that midnight would see the heavens burst open, with all believers ascending into glory, while sinners would be left behind on a planet swallowed by fire.

On that apocalyptic morning of April 3, in the Massachusetts town of Westford, a group of enthusiastic Millerites gathered inside the famous Bancroft Mansion, where they sat and discussed which hilltop they should assemble upon for their glorious midnight ascension into Heaven. It was the village idiot, an indigent known as Crazy Amos, who proved himself wiser than most that day. Securing for himself an old trumpet, the mischievous Amos positioned himself outside the mansion on the front lawn. He put the horn to his lips and let out several majestic blasts. Then, he sat back and enjoyed the show: dozens of Millerites tumbled out of windows and doors, thinking that the trumpet they had heard was the summons of the angel Gabriel! As frantic Millerites continued to pour out of the mansion, throwing themselves to the ground and shouting "Hallelujah! God has come for us!", Crazy Amos no longer felt alone in his role as village idiot.

In the meantime, on that fateful April 3, with the world about to end, the messenger of doom himself, William Miller, was comfortably reposing at his luxurious Massachusetts farm. Curiously, even though the minister had assured his followers that the world would surely end on that day, he had just installed 40 rods of new stone fencing on his property. This project, no doubt, had been financed by the enormous collections of diamonds, gold, and cash that had been taken up at various Millerite meetings.

April 3, 1843, passed without the apocalyptic cataclysm predicted by Miller. Still, his thousands of followers remained steadfast in their belief that the end was near, for their prophet had originally said that the final hour of reckoning would occur between March 21, 1843 and March 21, 1844. The Massachusetts minister reassured his flock that March 21,

1844, could not pass without the awesome event taking place. Enthusiastic devotees continued to give up homes and property, although, for reasons never explained, Miller himself continued to repose at his comfortable Massachusetts estate, meticulously maintaining his fields, constructing new fencing, and adding livestock to his holdings. Considering his claims that the entire world—presumably including his farm—would be reduced to ashes within a few months, the minister's home improvements were just a bit curious. Still, his fanatical followers didn't seem to notice.

Time passed, and God still hadn't kept his appointment with Miller. Then, the final day arrived: March 21, 1844. The minister had assured his devotees that the monumental event could happen no later than this date. Millerites once again donned their flowing white robes and gathered at cemeteries and on hilltops throughout the east, singing and praying, eagerly anticipating a rapturous elevator ride into Heaven.

In the freezing March night, thousands of cold, wet, and shivering Millerites stared upward to Heaven, expecting a sudden burst of fire that would herald the end. The only fire, however, was the one burning in the fireplace of Miller's Massachusetts manor house, where he was spending his last night on Earth comfortably toasting his toes by the hearth. Finally, midnight passed, and it became apparent that God had stood Miller up. "Slowly and silently the groups disbanded, their eyes filled with tears, their hearts heavy. Their white robes were soiled and torn; they were hungry and exhausted. But where could they go? They had no homes or worldly goods and were now faced with the urgency of finding food, clothing, and shelter, for the bitter winds of March did not share their fanatical faith," wrote one historian.

Within a few days, Miller announced that he had made a slight error in calculating the end of mankind. He had used the Gregorian calendar when he should have used the Jewish one; in reality, the awesome event would actually take place, this time for certain, on October 22, 1844. Incredibly, not only did his followers accept his explanation, but hundreds of new converts were added to their numbers! The great day of reckoning was CERTAIN to take place in October 22, and Miller warned all sinners that God was sure to flambé them unless they were prepared for His arrival!

The evening of October 22 saw a repetition of the events of March 21. Throughout New England and other parts of the east, thousands of Millerites flocked to cemeteries and hilltops in their white robes, where they sang and prayed late into the cold, wet night, while Miller once again saw fit to spend the apocalypse comfortably by his fireplace.

By morning, the world was still very much intact, though it now contained a good many more disillusioned people than usual. Instead of finding themselves in Heaven, Miller's followers found themselves in abject poverty. They had given up homes, property, and family for naught; many went insane, and many more committed suicide.

For the next five years, Miller lived as a recluse, slowly losing both his sight and his mind. In 1849, on his death-bed, Miller cried, "Victory! At last I see him!", and God, five years late, carried the old fraud away.

119

CERTAIN VERY INTERESTING
DEAD PEOPLE

A recent contract with a publisher for *The New England Ghost Files—Book II* has me back chasing ghosts, and I often find myself investigating various cemeteries that are purported sites of spectral activity.

More often than not, nothing about these various cemeteries suggests to me that they're haunted; yet these numerous treks to New England graveyards have not been for naught, for I have found that many of these sites offer something far more interesting than ghosts; namely, certain very interesting dead people.

It first happened at Oak Grove Cemetery in Fall River. I inadvertently stumbled upon the not-very-conspicuous gravestones of Andrew and Abby Borden, along with the stone of their daughter—and presumed murderer—Lizbeth, known to history as Lizzie. In an instant, the significance of my discovery struck me: here, on the very spot where I now was, Lizzie had once stood as her murdered parents were buried. I was sharing the very same physical space that a century earlier had been occupied by perhaps one of New England's most diabolical women; on this very ground where I now was, Lizzie had stood on that August afternoon of the funeral in 1892, perhaps in possession of an awful, hideous bit of knowledge about her parents' deaths which she was entirely unable to share with the other mourners present.

120

It was a generally neat kind of feeling, sharing identical physical space—and only a century between us—with such a celebrated gal.

And it eventually occurred again as my ghost book investigations took me to other important area cemeteries. I inadvertently stumbled upon the gravestones or tombs of such New England notables as Emily Dickinson (West Cemetery, Amherst), H. P. Lovecraft (Swan Point Cemetery, Providence), Jack Kerouac (Edison Cemetery, Lowell); and Harriet Beecher Stowe (Andover Chapel Cemetery, Andover). Such was the thrill of meeting in the flesh (or what once was flesh) the actual persons (or what once was persons) of some of my favored historical and cultural icons, that I began, when researching an alleged ghost report at any New England cemetery, to also query cemetery attendants as to whether or not I would find any New England notables planted in the immediate vicinity.

In time, I had assembled a rather colorful list. Perhaps there are those among you who, like myself, might enjoy meeting, albeit posthumously, some of your favored historical and cultural idols and icons. All are buried in Massachusetts and Rhode Island cemeteries:

Name	Fame / Burial Site
John Winthrop (d. 1649)	Mass. Bay Colony King's Chapel Burial Ground, Boston
Paul Revere (d. 1818)	Rode to alert minutemen Granary Burial Ground, Boston
John Hancock (d. 1793)	Declaration of Independence Granary Burial Ground, Boston

Samuel Adams (d. 1803)	Second Governor, Mass. Granary Burial Ground, Boston
Mary Goose (d. 1757)	"Mother Goose" Granary Burial Ground, Boston
Gilbert Stuart (d. 1828)	Portrait of Washington Central Burial Ground, Boston
Cotton Mather (d. 1728)	Salem Witch Trials Copp's Hill Burial Ground, Boston
Sacco/Vanzetti (d. 1927)	Executed Anarchists Forest Hills Cem., Boston
Arthur Fiedler (d. 1979)	Boston Pops St. Joseph's Cem., West Roxbury
Joseph P. Kennedy (d. 1969)	Kennedy Patriarch Holyhood Cem., Brookline
Henry Wadsworth Longfellow (d. 1882)	Poet Mt. Auburne Cem., Cambridge
Winslow Homer (d. 1910)	Artist Mt. Auburne Cem., Cambridge
Mary Baker Eddy (d. 1910)	Christian Science Mt. Auburne Cem., Cambridge
Henry James (d. 1916)	Novelist City of Cambridge Cem., Cambridge
John Quincy Adams (d. 1848)	President United First Parish Church, Quincy

Ralph Waldo Emerson (d. 1882) Writer
Sleepy Hollow Cem., Concord

Nathaniel Hawthorne (d. 1864) Writer
Sleepy Hollow Cem., Concord

Henry David Thoreau (d. 1862) Writer
Sleepy Hollow Cem., Concord

Louisa May Alcott (d. 1888) Writer
Sleepy Hollow Cem., Concord

Albert DeSalvo (d. 1973) Boston Strangler
Puritan Lawn Cem., Peabody

Harriet Beecher Stowe (d. 1896) Writer
Andover Chapel Cem., Andover

Jack Kerouac (d. 1969) Beat Writer, "On the Road"
Edison Cem., Lowell

Daniel Webster (d. 1852) Orator
Winslow Burying Ground, Marshfield

Miles Standish (d. 1656) Pilgrim Leader
Miles Standish Burial Ground, Duxbury

Lizzie Borden (d. 1927) Ax Murderess
Oak Grove Cem., Fall River

John Belushi (d. 1982) Comedian
Abel's Hill Cem., Martha's Vineyard

Clara Barton (d. 1912) Red Cross Founder
North Oxford Cem., Oxford

Emily Dickinson (d. 1886)	Poet West Cem., Amherst
Norman Rockwell (d. 1978)	Painter Stockbridge Cem., Stockbridge
Roger Williams (d. 1683)	R.I. Founder Prospect Terrace, Providence
Sarah Helen Whitman (d. 1878)	Lover of E. A. Poe North Burial Ground, Providence
Thomas Wilson Dorr	Dorr's Rebellion Swan Point Cem., Providence
H. P. Lovecraft	Horror Writer Swan Point Cem., Providence

THE NEW ENGLANDER
WHO DISCOVERED LIFE ON MARS

It was first announced in Boston. A New England astronomer, and a competent one at that, declared in 1894 that he had discovered irrefutable proof of life on Mars. He soon released a book about this amazing discovery and created a sensation. A good many people, some noted scientists among them, fully accepted the astronomer's unarguable "proof." The astronomer's astounding findings even inspired a young writer named H. G. Wells to write a book about Martians, a book known today as *War of the Worlds.*

The astronomer in question was a feisty Bostonian named Percival Lowell. Born to a wealthy family in 1855, Percival soon proved himself a keen and intelligent lad. By the time he was 11, he was already composing poems in Latin and French. He went on to attend Harvard, where he graduated with honors. After spending a year abroad in Europe and the Near East, Percival returned to Boston to work for his wealthy grandfather. He managed trust funds and served as the treasurer of a cotton mill, soon accumulating a sizeable fortune. In 1883, deciding to take some time off to afford his inquisitive mind free reign, Percival traveled to Japan. The young man was so taken by the textured and colorful culture of the Orient that he returned there numerous times over the next ten years, writing several books about Japanese people and culture.

Among his many hobbies (botany, polo, hiking), astronomy was Percival's favorite. And being the wealthy young man that he was, Percival was in a position to make his favorite hobby a full-time occupation. In 1893, he had a sizeable observatory built in Flagstaff, Arizona (where the skies were relatively clear for viewing the cosmos), and from then on he spent his time between Boston and Flagstaff.

Percival was fascinated by the earlier observations of Giovanni Schiparelli, who, in 1877, had reported that there were a series of long, narrow, perfectly straight lines (which he dubbed "canali") criss-crossing the surface of Mars. From his observatory in Flagstaff, Percival and his two hired assistants closely studied the curious lines on Mars' surface (which could only be seen with a high-powered, quality telescope). Soon, the wealthy Bostonian concluded the obvious: this network of perfectly straight, symmetrical, intersecting lines on Mars could not represent natural phenomena.

In less than a year, the New Englander published his sensational book, *Mars*. In vivid prose Lowell described Mars as a dying world – a chilly, desert-like planet...and the true nature of the 'canali' (straight lines on the surface) was to him startling but obvious: "they were artificial waterways or canals, constructed thousands of years ago by the Martians in a desperate attempt to stave off extinction as water grew scarce and areas of sterile desert grew larger..." *(Those Eccentric Yankees, Camden, Maine: Yankee Books, 1991;4.)*

Lowell's startling book quickly reached a sizeable audience and created quite a stir. Mars became front page news throughout the country and generated a vigorous debate among leading astronomers. In the meantime, everyone and his brother scanned for Mars with whatever makeshift telescope they could find, even if it meant using an opera glass.

While some professional astronomers reacted to the New Englander's assertions scornfully, others entertained the possibility that Lowell just might be correct in his assumptions of an ancient Martian civilization. A dispute ensued in the scientific journals. In not so many words, the feisty and sarcastic Lowell intimated that those who disagreed with him probably did so because they were idiots, or at least because they weren't using the proper equipment to observe the planet in question.

In 1906, Lowell followed up his first book with another, entitled *Mars and Its Canals.* Two years later, he wrote *Mars as the Abode of Life.* "Lowell's reasons for believing Mars to be inhabited were put forward so persuasively that in 1907, the *Wall Street Journal,* not ordinarily noted for its quick acceptance of radical ideas, asserted that the most important event of the previous year was Lowell's proof that life existed on Mars" *(Those Eccentric Yankees, Camden, Maine: Yankee Books, 1991; 7.)*

Lowell's books enjoyed immense popularity, and he next turned his attention to another curious celestial project. From his observatory in Flagstaff, the sky-gazing Bostonian observed irregularities in the orbit of Uranus and Neptune and concluded that another celestial body must be exerting gravitational pull. Using a series of complex mathematical equations and tedious sequential photography, Lowell concluded that an unknown planet, a celestial body he dubbed "Planet X," orbited somewhere beyond Neptune. He worked on the project for years, though he never directly sighted the elusive planet he was so certain existed.

Lowell died convinced that there was, indeed, a distant, unknown "Planet X" at the outer perimeter of the solar system. As for the "Martian Canals" supposedly constructed by aliens, the flybys of the spaceprobe "Mariner," long after Lowell's death, proved his Martian theory completely erroneous in 1969 and 1971. Close-up photographs of Mars' surface showed that the "canals" were actually craters, valleys, and dry river beds which, viewed at the great distance from which Lowell had observed them, created an optical illusion of straight, symmetrical lines on the planet's surface.

Thus, the New Englander had not, after all, discovered proof of life on Mars, a premise to which he had devoted most of his life. Yet, his later calculations of a "Planet X" somewhere beyond Neptune, a planet whose existence he suspected but which he never actually saw, were a bit more important in the annals of astronomical inquiry. The Bostonian, in fact, had set the stage for discovery of the planet Pluto, as later confirmed by astronomer Clyde Tombaugh in 1930, after Lowell's death.

THE STRANGER IN THE FOREST

The Providence Literary Cadet of June, 1826, relates an intriguing account of an eccentric hermit who, beginning about 1806 and continuing for over twenty years, lived a strange and solitary life in Seekonk, Massachusetts (a portion of Seekonk that is now part of East Providence) at the bank of the Seekonk River. Interestingly, this reclusive character was not a typical vagrant but was, according to the local residents who sometimes encountered him, "remarkably abstemious, and otherwise correct in his habits, never known to be guilty of profanity, civil and agreeable in his manners, and polite to all who visited him...".

Let us try to determine who this hermit really was, and why—for over two decades—he withdrew from the world into the Seekonk woods.

The recluse, known as Robert, occupied a rude and secluded hut that he had constructed in a pine grove on the east side of the Seekonk River, near India Bridge (on land owned at that time by the Hon. Tristam Berges, who had apparently granted Robert permission to reside quietly on his vast wooded estate).

A description of Robert and his hermitage, recorded by a writer named Henry Trumbull in 1829, reads as follows:

> *Robert is apparently sixty years of age (as of 1829),*
> *twenty-one years after first building a hermitage at*
> *the banks of the Seekonk River. A little short of six*

feet in height, inclined to corpulency, his features perfectly regular, and of a complexion a shade or two darker...than that of whites. In his early years he states that his skin was much more fair, but of late years, having been so much exposed to the smoke of his small cell (or hut), has become much changed. The lower part of his face is covered with a thick and curly beard, of a jet black, and of uncommon length: his garments, or many of them, are of his own manufacture....

The walls of his cave or cell are constructed principally of round stones of inconsiderable size, rudely thrown together...and although they form a square of thirty or forty feet in circumference, yet are so thick and massy, as to enclose only a single apartment of not sufficient size to contain more than two or three persons at a time, and so low as to not admit of their standing erect, and indeed is in every respect of much less comfortable construction than many of our pig pens. At the center there is a fireplace rudely formed, from which proceeds a flue in the form of a chimney; and at the extreme end of his cell Robert has constructed a berth or bunk, in which, filled with rags and straw, he reposes at night. Besides the fire place stands a block, made of oak, which serves him for a seat and table. The hut is decorated with various shells and bones, and sits on the declivity of a wooded hill (in a pine grove), overlooking the pellucid waters of the Seekonk River.

In cooking utensils Robert is quite deficient; the one half of an iron pot is the only article made use of by him, in which he prepares his food. A small piece of iron hoop serves him for a knife, and a few articles of damaged delftware, and an old sea bucket for the conveyance of water from a nearby spring.

To his gloomy cell there are but one or two apertures or loopholes, for the admission of light, which in winter are completely closed, as is every crack and crevice, with seaweed. This renders the apartment still more dark and gloomy. Robert remains within, day and night, in almost total darkness. In summer, Robert employs a considerable portion of his time in the cultivation of a small spot of ground, contiguous to his hut, of 7 or 8 rods square. The soil is so barren and unproductive, that it seldom produces annually more than three for four bushels of potatoes, a peck or two of corn, and a few quarts of beans...

Robert was in possession of a Bible...said he never doubted the existence of a Supreme Being. From this belief he said he derived great consolation for, although great had been his trials and troubles in this world, he was not without hope that by complying with the terms of the gospel, he might be permitted in another world to participate in eternal enjoyments.

From *"Life and Adventures of Robert The Hermit,"* a small pamphlet written and published by Henry Trumbull in 1829.

Who was Robert the Hermit, and why had he decided to so fully withdraw from the ordinary world for over two decades— from circa 1808 to the time of his death (probably circa early 1830's)? From the accounts of various local people who visited the amiable recluse during his years of solitary Seekonk residency (including some, like Henry Trumbull, who made written notes concerning this mysterious character), it becomes clear that Robert withdrew from life because, quite simply, life had irreparably broken his heart.

Trumbull's extensive interview with the Seekonk hermit in the 1820's (published in 1829 as a small pamphlet entitled, as we have already indicated, "Life and Adventures of Robert The Hermit") relates the following facts:

• Robert was born at Princeton, New Jersey, in 1769 or 1770. As his mother was of African descent, Robert was born a slave.

• At the age of four, Robert was profoundly traumatized by being sold to another master who took him to Georgetown, D.C., thus separating Robert from his mother and sister forever.

• In 1789, at the age of 19, Robert fell in love with a young woman named Alley Pennington. Hoping to spend his life with her as a free man, Robert won his master's promise that he could buy his own freedom for the sum of fifty pounds.

• A professed friend of Robert's—a free white man

by the name of James Bevens, paid the fifty pounds in full to Robert's master, on the condition that the bill of sale should remain in his hands until such time as Robert, by the fruits of his industry, should be able to repay Bevens the principal and interest.

• While Robert worked diligently to repay Bevens so that he could quickly earn his freedom, he married his love Alley Pennington. The couple soon had two children.

• Robert worked at various odd jobs and paid each day's wages to Bevens. He got closer and closer to paying off the debt in full. As he trusted Bevens implicitly, he never asked for receipts for these payments. That was a mistake, for when the amount was finally paid in full, Bevens did not grant Robert his freedom as promised.

• Instead, Bevens had Robert pinioned and chained, dragged him away from his beloved wife and children, and sold him to the southern slave market sometime around 1791. Robert was sold at auction but managed to escape and secret himself in the cargo hold of a ship bound for Philadelphia. However, he was soon discovered by the crew, was returned to his master, and was subsequently sold to a Dr. Peter Fersue.

• In time, Robert managed to escape again, this time secreting himself on a sloop bound for Philadelphia.

• The stow-away Robert was eventually discovered by the ship's crew once again, but, the ship's captain being a Quaker opposed to slavery, he allowed

Robert to go free once the ship landed in Boston.

• Realizing that it was far too dangerous to return to the South to find his wife and children, Robert set up his home in Salem, Massachusetts, remarried, and worked for many years as a sailor on cargo ships bound from Salem for India. The work was prosperous and, as Robert was fairly light-skinned as a mulatto, no one seemed to suspect that he was a runaway slave.

• One month, upon returning to Salem from one of his jobs on a cargo ship, he was suddenly and unexpectedly told by his wife that she no longer loved him and wanted no more to do with him. Robert was never able to account for this dramatic change in his spouse. Broken-hearted, he never saw her again.

• About 1808, Robert decided that since nearly twenty years had passed, it might now be safe for him to return to the South without being recognized as a runaway slave. His aim was to find out what became of his beloved Alley Pennington, his first wife, and their two children. Although Robert was not recognized nor re-apprehended upon his return to the South, he did learn that, shortly after he had been so brutally torn away from her some twenty years earlier, his wife Alley had committed suicide in a state of profound despair, and that her helpless babies had not long survived her.

• It was at this point, Robert decided, that he would retreat from a world that had been so ruthlessly cruel to him. He returned north by ship to Rhode

Island and built his first secluded hut in 1808 on uninhabited land (Fox Point) situated about one mile south of Providence Bridge. However, local youths began to harass the recluse after a few years. Hence, in about 1811, he relocated his hut—with the permission of land owner Hon. Tristam Burges—to the wooded pine grove on the hill overlooking the east bank of the Seekonk River, where he would spend the rest of his days in that part of Seekonk (a portion now incorporated into East Providence).

During his many years in his Seekonk hermitage, Robert was visited by curious local youths and adults. Trumbull noted that Robert was "always willing to gratify the curiosity of such people as feel disposed to inspect the internal part of his cell." Trumbull also notes that many visitors brought various gifts to the likeable hermit (including books, for Robert loved to spend much of his time reading). Trumbull added that visitors came to Robert's secluded abode for a taste of the romantic and unusual. Trumbull says:

Robert's cell is surrounded by a thick-set hedge wrought of wild briars and hemlock, and displays much ingenuity and taste. It is a most romantic situation, some distance from any human habitation. To visit it is well worth the trouble of those who are fond of the curious, and are pleased with noticing the eccentricities of frail mortality... for they all love poor Robert.

Indeed, after so many years of peacefully residing in their woods—disturbing no one and hospitably entertaining anyone who called upon him—Robert had apparently won the hearts of the townsfolk. In his last sickness he was comfortably provided for by the Selectmen of Seekonk, and, upon his death (apparently in the early 1830's), his burial costs were assumed by the town.

CHAPTER FOUR

NEW ENGLAND ENIGMAS

BOSTON'S MYSTERIOUS SKELETON IN CHAINS

In 1905, three workmen were repairing part of the old Independence Fort on Castle Island in Boston Harbor. Instructed to repair an old dungeon in the fort's cellar, the men descended a dark and musty stone staircase by torchlight. When they reached the cellar, the men were surprised to find that there was no dungeon, even though it was clearly marked on the fort's plans. Where the dungeon was supposed to be, there was only a brick wall.

The men brought the matter to the attention of the supervisor, who instructed them to break down the wall. For hours, the men hammered away until they finally broke through. When they did, what they saw made them gasp.

Behind the mysterious wall, the men found the small dungeon. And within the dungeon there was an ancient skeleton chained to the floor. The implications were apparent. The victim had been placed into the dungeon and had been walled in alive. He had been sealed in to die.

The workmen didn't know it at the time, but they had stumbled upon an extremely important piece of literary history. Many years earlier, a young soldier by the name of Edgar Allen Poe had been stationed at the very same Boston fort. And years later he would write a short tale called *The Cask of Amontillado*—which would become one of his most famous short stories. In fact, his macabre tale was about a man being walled-up alive!

Is it just coincidence that Edgar Allen Poe had been stationed at the fort where a gruesome walling-in had actually taken place? Or did he somehow know about it? Was Poe's *The Cask of Amontillado*—which is set in Europe—actually based on a Boston incident?

Private Poe was sent to Fort Independence in 1827, at the age of 18. It is said that he became fascinated by a lonely marble gravestone situated just outside the walls of the fort. An inscription on the stone read as follows:

> *Beneath this stone are deposited the remains of Lieut. Robert F. Massie, of the U.S. Regt. of Light Artillery. Near this spot on the 25th, Decr, 1817 fell Lieut. Robert F. Massie, Aged 21 years.*

Curious as to how Lieut. Massie had been killed within the safety of a fort, Poe allegedly interviewed almost every soldier stationed there. Soon, the grisly account began to unfold.

Ten years earlier, in 1817, Robert Massie arrived at Fort Independence from Virginia. The young officer got on well with the other soldiers stationed there, though there was one officer, a Captain Green, who took a violent dislike to him. Green was something of a bully, and he was also an expert swordsman.

One December evening, the fort officers were playing cards. Young Massie laid down his hand, and Captain Green suddenly sprang to his feet, slapped Massie square in the face, and accused him of cheating. Demanding satisfaction, he then

141

challenged the young lieutenant to a duel. Massie, though he knew he hadn't been cheating, wished to preserve his honor and reputation. He accepted Captain Green's challenge.

Fearing for the young lieutenant's life, the other officers urged Captain Green to call off the duel. Young Massie was no match for the seasoned captain's expert swordsmanship. Still, the aggressive officer ignored their pleas. The duel took place on Christmas morning.

Indeed, young Massie was at a great disadvantage. Almost immediately, he was run through by Green's sword. The other officers carried his body to the outer walls of the fort, where he was buried.

For several weeks afterward, ill sentiment against Captain Green ran high. Then, the officer suddenly vanished. Eventually, military officials concluded that Green had deserted, and they wrote him off the records.

However, a few of the men at the fort knew that Captain Green hadn't deserted at all. In fact, he had been walled up alive. Several soldiers, outraged by young Massie's death, had abducted the captain and had chained him in the fort's tiny dungeon. Then, they sealed up the dungeon with a brick wall, leaving Captain Green to die a horrible, suffocating death. As the dungeon was no longer in use, Green's body would remain undiscovered for years.

And thus, Edgar Allen Poe learned of the gruesome events of ten years earlier. Supposedly, the young writer was enthralled, and he made many notes about the incident. It is said that Poe was eventually reprimanded by the Fort's commanding officer for taking such an unusual and morbid interest in the occurrence. Tradition has it that he was instructed to never relate what he had learned to anyone outside the fort.

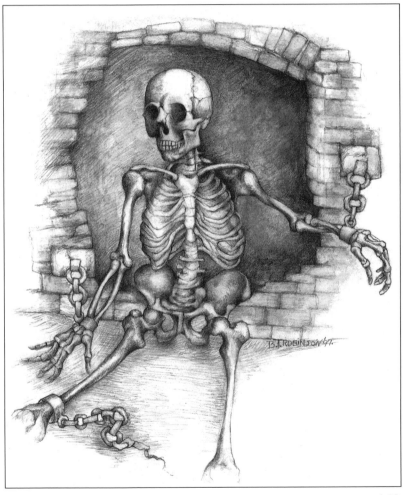

Poe never told anyone about the dark secret of Fort Independence. Years later, however, he wrote his renowned short story, *The Cask of Amontillado*, in which the main character is walled up alive and left to die a horrific death. While Poe may have changed the characters and the setting, some historians believe that his story—one of the world's most famous—was directly inspired by the terrible events in Boston.

After the discovery of his chained skeleton in 1905, Captain Green was afforded a military funeral and was buried in the fort cemetery. As for the remains of Lieutenant Massie, they were relocated several times and were finally interred at Fort Devons in Ayer, Massachusetts, in 1939. To this day, there seems to be a good deal of secrecy and lore surrounding Captain Green's terrible death, a death that likely inspired one of Edgar Allen Poe's most disturbing and haunting short stories.

MYSTERIOUS MISCELLANY

The following four New England accounts—all of them quite "over the edge"—represent a short compilation of odd historical facts, bizarre occurrences, and inexplicable phenomena, all of which are supposedly factual.

These strange reports—which derive from regional newspaper accounts, town histories, and various other published sources, both historical and modern—cover four instances of varied New England weirdness; in short, the sort of stuff that I shouldn't be writing about if I want to be taken seriously as a researcher.

But fun is fun.

I make no attempt to either prove or disprove any of these unusual New England events. The reader is invited to make up his or her own mind concerning their prospective validity. I myself draw no firm conclusions about these curious reports. In my own mind, I merely file them under "H" (for "Huh?")

I myself am very skeptical of UFO's, but I find the following account intriguing, nonetheless:

Colonial Close Encounters

In March of 1639, long before the advent of aircraft or other man-made flying objects with which UFO's are often confused, James Everall and two companions made America's first documented UFO sighting in colonial Boston. Purportedly, the three Massachusetts colonists observed a startling, immense flying light in the sky near Muddy River. Their description, which was recorded and survives to this day, mentions a great light in the sky which, *"when it stood still (hovered), it flamed up, and appeared about three yards square, and when it ran, it contracted into (a strange) figure...".*

James Everall and his two companions, thoroughly startled by the strange experience, made a formal report to John Winthrop, Governor of the colony. Winthrop, who considered the strange incident significant and credible enough to record it in writing, described Everall as "a sober, discreet man." In his journal, Winthrop writes that Everall observed the flying object *"run swift as an arrow towards Charleston, and so up and down for about two or three hours. Other credible people saw the same light, after, at about the same place...."*

The object's strange back and forth motion over a period of "two or three hours" seems to rule out a comet or meteor. No explanation for the curious light in the sky was ever determined.

A Massachusetts Monster Mystery

Despite thousands of reported sightings by sailors and even reliable ship's officers over the past few hundred years, the notion of giant, serpent-like sea creatures occasionally poking their heads from dark, uncharted depths strikes most of us as rather silly. And yet, some oceanographers and zoologists acknowledge that the world's oceans, representing an immense portion of the planet's surface, undoubtedly contain numerous species of life that are completely unknown to us, given the many miles of ocean depth that remain entirely unexplored.

For instance, in the early 1970's, Japanese fishermen accidently netted a large, bizarre, armor-plated fish resembling nothing they had previously encountered. When the specimen was transported to a university for analysis, scientists determined that it was actually a living example of a very ancient "dinosaur" fish thought to have been extinct for many tens of millions of years. The immense size and staggering depth of the ocean had prevented—until now—any encounters with or knowledge of this primitive, armor-plated sea creature.

Might we wonder, then, if the strange, immense, serpent-like creature sighted by numerous credible witnesses off the coast of Massachusetts in the 19th-century was an unknown species of giant something (??) that had found its way to the New England coastline from some remote and distant part of the ocean? As suggested by at least one scientist, could the monster, given its reptilian appearance and striking resemblance to the plesiosaur family of dinosaur, have actually been a living specimen of plesiosaur, an immense ocean reptile thought (perhaps mistakenly?) to have been extinct for tens of millions of years?

When the Massachusetts sea serpent first made its appearance in 1815 off of Gloucester, witnesses to the sighting did not consist merely of a few drunken fishermen. Rather, as the strange, 80-foot snake-like creature began frolicking up and down the northern Massachusetts coastline, some 500 people, many of them reputable and reliable, testified to seeing the serpent week after week—first off Gloucester, then off Lynn, Swampscott, Salem, and Nahant, all along the Massachusetts north shore, and then farther north off the coast of Maine.

One of the first witnesses to observe the strange creature, a gentleman from Cape Anne named Amos Stury, offered the following testimony to the New England Linnean Society, which investigated the sightings: *"I have often seen many whales at sea, but this animal was much swifter than any whale. He had a head like a serpent (something like the head of a rattlesnake, but nearly as large as the head of a horse)...."*

Another apparently reliable witness was Thomas Perkins (a respectable social figure who founded the Perkins Institute for the Blind in Boston). Perkins, who was among the earliest group of witnesses who sighted the monster off Gloucester, gave the following testimony: *"The (creature) moved with rapid motion up the harbor on the western shore. As it approached us, it was easy to see that its motion was not that of a common snake...but rather was evidently the vertical movement of the caterpillar...I had a fine glass...and (saw that) the head was flat in the water and the animal was, as far as I could distinguish, of a chocolate color. I was struck with an appearance in the front part of the head, like a single horn, about nine inches to a foot in length, and of the form of a marling-spike. There was a great many people collected by this time, many of whom had before seen the same object and the same appearance. From the time I first saw it, until it passed by the place where I stood, and soon after it disappeared, was not more than fifteen minutes. I left fully satisfied that the*

148

reports in circulation...were essentially correct."

Other witnesses included a Mr. and Mrs. Mansfield, well-respected citizens of Gloucester, who said that while taking a carriage drive by the beach near the harbor, they witnessed a *"serpent stretched out in shallow water with its tail on the white sand and its head in deeper water."*

Additional sightings took place all along the northern Massachusetts and northern New England coastline throughout the summer of 1815, with an eventual total, as previously indicated, of some 500 witnesses. And then, toward the end of the summer, the serpent disappeared from coastal waters as suddenly as it had appeared.

But not for good. The creature purportedly reappeared off the Massachusetts coast in 1819, with additional sightings in 1820, 1823, 1826 and even later. The reports of later years, however, by which time there had undoubtedly emerged a growing body of folklore surrounding the original sightings of 1815, might represent nothing more than "copycat" sightings. It is the original appearance of the creature in the summer of 1815— with some 500 witnesses to the event (including Samuel Cabot, a respected ancestor of Henry Cabot Lodge)—that stirs the greatest amount of wonder.

Descriptions of the serpent seem to rule out a whale or a giant squid. The precise species identification of the sinuous, 80-foot sea creature remains, to this day, a mystery.

River Spirits

*Note: The following is an updated, expanded version of an account that originally appeared in my book, **The New England Ghost Files** (1994: Covered Bridge Press).*

Several residents of Tiverton, Rhode Island, report witnessing a recurring nighttime apparition on the Sakonnet River, which flows into Narragansett Bay. On a few occasions over a twelve year period, a group of three canoes, carrying six Indians, has been observed silently making its way down the river in the moonlight.

Local witnesses—most of whom live near the river and seem sincerely affected by what they've seen—indicate that the canoes and their occupants are clearly not of this world, for the Indians' oars are observed to silently strike and penetrate the water with no sound or splash whatsoever, creating not even a ripple. When witnesses call out to the Indians, the ghosts quickly vanish, along with their canoes, into thin air—as if they've been startled or disturbed by the people calling out to them from the shoreline.

During one purported sighting on a July evening in 1984, three local residents watched in awe as the Native occupants of the canoes passionately threw their arms up to the sky, as though engaged in some sort of ritual, and then the Indians and their canoes suddenly vanished.

Recent Update: In early April 1996, a retired business owner and local resident, while taking a leisurely stroll along the river's edge with his adult daughter, purportedly noticed two Indian-manned canoes engaged in some sort of conflict out in the middle of the river. The canoes rammed each other aggressively while the Native occupants viciously swung at one another with stone-tipped clubs and axes. The man and his daughter indicate that the Indians were clearly wounding each other terribly, for their faces and bodies were streaming with blood. The entire apparition lasted for a surprisingly short period of time—merely five or six seconds. The canoes had suddenly appeared on the river in the midst of battle, only to quickly vanish again just moments later while the occupants were still engaged in combat.

Had some past aggressive incident at the river—perhaps one that took place hundreds of years earlier—become momentarily superimposed on the present in some sort of brief, inexplicable "time-warp" phenomenon? Do the various other Native American ghost sightings reported along this part of the Sakonnet River suggest that something from long ago is still very wrong or amiss there—perhaps unresolved human emotions involving Native Americans who once occupied the area (and may have engaged in occasional inter-tribal warfare along the river) many centuries ago? These very speculative questions will, of course, remain forever unanswered.

Archaeological surveys and artifactual recoveries along the Sakonnet River do, in fact, indicate that the river was extensively utilized by Native Americans during prehistoric and early historic times.

Strange Incident
At Fort Devens, Massachusetts

UFO reports are, in this writer's opinion, rarely to be taken seriously. However, the following New England incident, much more recent (1957) than the colonial account described earlier, seems to involve far too many reliable witnesses—most of them military personnel—to be lightly dismissed, although this doesn't mean that an extra-terrestrial explanation should be blindly embraced.

As described by Ellis Cahill, noted New England researcher and author of a number of books (including work for *National Geographic*), this strange occurrence possibly represents one of the most provocative New England UFO incidents on record.

In a recent publication, Cahill reports as follows: *One constant worry for the military is that many reliable sightings by multitudes of eye-witnesses center around military bases. At Fort Devons, Massachusetts, which houses an Army Security installation, eight 'flying saucers' were seen by hundreds of Army personnel and civilians for a period of one half-hour on the evening of September 17, 1957....The 'bright orange discs' were first seen traveling high in the sky from east to west, and at first there were only three of them. Then another was spotted going west to east, then three more passed over the army post, traveling south. They made no sound and there was no trailing vapor. One stopped and hovered about 5,000 feet above the ground, and another 'oscillated up and down.' They flew much faster than conventional aircraft. A fast call to Bedford Air*

152

Force Base revealed they had only one jet up in the air at the time, and it was flying far to the north of Fort Devens. These glowing saucers remained over the post for a long time, criss-crossing and changing directions and altitudes. Most of the personnel at Devens were told by their commanding officer to 'keep quiet' about what they saw. Were the UFO's some sort of experimental aircraft, or were they manned by extra-terrestrials who were curious about the various technological goings-on at Fort Devens?"

Many 'natural' explanations might explain the strange sightings on that September evening in 1957. Still, the appearance and peculiar aerial movements of the 'bright orange discs' do not seem to correlate with any known man-made flying objects.

Experimental human aircraft? Or extra-terrestrials curious about the military installation at Fort Devens? The true answer, like those for the other mysterious accounts presented in this chapter, remains an obscure New England enigma.

THE DAY IT RAINED FISH
A TRUE FISH STORY

Note: The following article by Mr. Robinson first appeared in **Yankee.**

On May 15, 1900, at about 4 P.M., Officer James Sullivan caught a fish. And he wasn't even fishing. As the Providence, Rhode Island policeman walked his beat in the Olneyville section of town, a four-inch pout fish suddenly dropped from the sky, landing just a few feet away from him on the cobblestone street.

Scratching his head, the perplexed policeman leaned over to pick up the wriggling creature. Indeed, something fishy was happening. Had some mischievous youngster, secretly perched upon a rooftop, tried to assault the unsuspecting policeman with a fish?

Officer Sullivan glanced upward, hoping to spot the culprit, when suddenly a second fish dropped inexplicably from the sky. And then, a few moments later, a whole shower of fish came raining down from the heavens: dozens and dozens of them—wet, wiggly, and still very much alive.

Officer Sullivan was not the only person in Olneyville to notice that it was raining fish. In fact, in that section of Providence, fish were pouring from the sky almost everywhere. On Harris Avenue, the fishing was even better. In a scene that would have stirred envy among even the most successful of Gloucester fisherman, people held out bins and buckets and caught literally hundreds of falling fish with unprecedented ease. And many people began to wonder: were the Biblical stories of manna raining down from the heavens really true after all? In "scaling" the issue, others looked to more practical explanations. That May afternoon of 1900 had been an unusually hot one—the hottest on record in over twenty years. But suddenly, at about 4 P.M., the temperature had dramatically dropped from 90 to 73 degrees in a matter of minutes. Winds quickly reached gale velocity, the sky grew ominously dark, and hail stones began to fall from above. In other words, meteorological conditions were ripe for a tornado.

While never officially spotted, it seemed likely that a tornado had sucked the ill-fated fishes from nearby ponds and lakes and had redeposited them, still very much alive, into the grasping hands of Olneyville's grateful residents, establishing a new all-time low in the price of fresh fish.

And while most of the people lucky enough to catch a falling fish were satisfied with their free seafood dinners, a few more enterprising individuals put their fishes to work for them. The proprietor of O'Garra's Saloon at the corner of Broadway and Valley Streets, realizing that such a curiosity would attract gawking customers, prominently displayed his specimen in a large tank and waited for word of his heaven-descended fish to get out.

Earlier that morning, before the unusual fish-fall had taken place, a weather forecast in the *Providence Journal* reported that May 15 would be "a day for the lightest of clothing, for the gorgeous outing shirt and for straw hats and cool drinks." A more accurate forecast should have perhaps gone something like this: "Warm and sunny in the morning, turning windy and cloudy by mid-afternoon, with a moderate chance of late afternoon fish."

THE MYSTERIOUS UNDERGROUND CHAMBER

Some 4,500 years ago, a small Late Archaic band of about twenty or thirty Indians began to camp in Rehoboth, Massachusetts, for a good part of the fall, not far from what is today the Rehoboth Village. Evidence suggests that they returned to the same general spot year after year. Their six-acre campsite was ideally located on a sandy plateau overlooking a sparkling, spring-fed stream (or, topographical evidence suggests, perhaps even a lake, long since dried up) that provided fresh water. The spot was a pleasant one for the season, with a nice dry elevation and lush surrounding woods in which the band hunted birds and found flavorful hickory nuts for later roasting by the evening fires. A short walk away was the Palmer River, where some of the Indians could launch their canoes and navigate to hunting areas deeper within the forest, while others back at the campsite skinned animal hides with stone scrapers, readying the skins for use as clothing in preparation for the impending winter.

Until several years ago, this Rehoboth campsite was obscurely hidden away under centuries of wind-deposited soil layers. Aside from an occasional time-worn arrowhead or burned hearth stone making its way to the modern-day surface, the site was a barren, sandy knoll that gave little indication of its ancient occupation.

Yet the human activities that took place on this spot several millennia ago have become discernible. Through careful archaeological excavation, some of the buried tools, weapons, and even foodstuffs of these Archaic people have once again seen the light of day. Under analysis, these fragments of Rehoboth prehistory have begun to tell an ages-old story of successful human survival in a wilderness setting. Especially intriguing is a curious, partially underground chamber.

In 1986, the Cohannet Chapter of the Massachusetts Archaeological Society initiated controlled excavations, under the direction of Brady Fitts of Raynham. At this time, the site was formally named the Tobey Site, after the property owners, Mr. and Mrs. Paul Tobey.

Excavations continued periodically for the next five years. Eventually, Fitts and his team of researchers uncovered numerous stone artifacts and site features. Carbon dating of associated charcoal indicated that the Archaic occupation of this ancient Rehoboth site began at least as early as 2,700 B.C.

In the present writer's opinion, the site was likely used for fall encampments. The discovery of charred hickory nuts and bird bones points to occupations at fall time, when these foods would have been plentiful, while the complete absence of fish bone seems to preclude spring or summer occupations. Additionally, stone fire hearths (for warmth) were too few in number to suggest occupations during winter. Thus, the site was probably used, perhaps year after year, as an autumn stopover by a band of Archaic Indians who may have left some nearby seasonal summer fishing camp with the coming of fall and who were on their way to winter hunting grounds further inland, where small winter game was most prevalent—away from the cold winter winds of the seaside. Fitts and his assistants excavated the site using a grid layout system. After some sixty squares (each one square meter in size) had been opened, a number of notable features came to light. For instance, three cooking hearths were unearthed; these were roughly circular arrangements of stones (found disturbed and somewhat scattered, probably by frost action) that contained charcoal and other evidence of having once contained fires. As noted above, Fitts and his team also found nearby remnants of charred hickory nuts and bird bones, indicating that the camp's occupants had sat around the hearths roasting these foods.

At another section of the site, excavators unearthed a high concentration of stone scraping tools. Undoubtedly, once scraped clean, the hides were subsequently used for clothing and for shelter covering. (Shelters at the campsite consisted of brush or sapling frameworks, over which animal skins were stretched for protection against the elements.) At least thirty such stone hide scrapers were found in this part of the camp.

In other sections of the site, Fitts and his team recovered numerous projectile points, a sharpening stone, a crude plummet, and stone anvils for cracking nuts. In total, over 1,000 stone artifacts were unearthed. Undoubtedly the most mysterious discovery made at Rehoboth's Tobey Site was the unearthing of what seems to be a sweat lodge, a partially subterranean enclosure that the camp's inhabitants may have utilized as a sort of heated "sauna," to cleanse the skin and perhaps also for certain types of purification ritual. Fitts describes finding the remains of a circular structure, about fourteen feet in diameter and with a small entrance, which had been built partially underground. The above-ground portion of the structure, he suggests, had probably consisted of a sapling frame roof covered with mud and leaves. At the center of the underground portion of the enclosure Fitts found a scooped-out fire pit, which, he postulates, may have been used to illuminate the interior of the structure or to hold a smudge fire that would repel mosquitoes. He also discovered a small platform or seat near this central fireplace which may have been occupied by the person who tended the fire pit.

Immediately adjacent to the remains of the structure, Fitts found a large number of buried stones, which, he believes, were heated outside and were then brought into the structure to warm it to a suitable level for "sweating." Once the stones were inside, the occupants of the lodge likely threw water on them to generate steam.

Later colonial accounts of Indian sweat lodges give us some idea of how this earlier Archaic example may have been utilized. One colonial observer noted the following:

> *They were made as a vault, partly underground, and in the form of a large oven, where two or three persons might on occasion sit together...and their method was to heat stones very hot in the fire, and put them into the (sweat lodge), and when the persons were in, to shut it close up with only so much air as was necessary for respiration...and being thus closely pent up, the heat of the stones occasioned them to sweat in a prodigious manner, streaming as it were from every part of their body, and when they had continued there for as long as*

*they could well endure it, their method was to rush
out and plunge themselves into (some nearby)
water. By this means they (seek) a cure of all pains
and numbness in their joints and many other
maladies.*

Samuel Niles (1760)

Roger Williams has also left us with an account of local Indian
sweat lodges:

*...they had exceedingly heated it with store of wood,
laid upon an heape of stones in the middle. When
they had taken out the fire, the stones keep still a
great heat...(the men) enter at once starke
naked...here do they sit around their hot stones an
houre or more...discoursing and sweating together;
which seating they use for two ends: First to
cleanse their skin: Secondly to purge their bodies,
which doubtless is a great means of preserving
them, and recovering them from diseases....*

Williams (1643)

While Rehoboth's sweat lodge dates to a much earlier period (a
radiocarbon date from charcoal taken from the lodge dates it to
about 2,700 B.C.), its general construction suggests that it was
probably utilized in very much the same manner as those
structures described in the accounts presented above. What
these colonial writers were possibly observing, then, was the
continuation of an ancient tradition that dated back to the much
earlier Archaic period, as suggested by the presence of the
sweat lodge at Rehoboth's Tobey Site. Such a finding at an

Archaic site is unique in New England, and, for this reason especially, excavations at the Tobey Site represent an important contribution to the archaeological study of this region.

Artist's conception of Rehoboth's mysterious and very ancient underground chamber—or "sweat lodge."

MYSTERIOUS STONE CHAMBER

Archaeological research has revealed that New England was, for millennia, profusely populated by Indians. However, a small number of historians and archaeologists suggest that the Indians of this region were not culturally isolated. Some researchers, in fact, controversially postulate that ancient seafarers of European origin traversed the Atlantic and established several small New England settlements, perhaps as early as 2,000 B.C.

In Norton, Massachusetts, there stands an enigmatic stone "chamber" which is currently under archaeological investigation. Ken Moore, an amateur archaeologist who directs the Norton study and who has presented his findings on local television, dismisses any notions that the curious structure may be colonial. The elaborate and distinctive construction of the Norton chamber, he maintains, has identical correlations at Celtic archaeological sites in Europe. He also notes that quarry marks appearing on the structure's stones defy colonial typology. Additionally, he and his small team of researchers have unearthed what they believe is evidence of ritual activity and human burial at the site, precluding, says Moore, the possibility of colonial origin.

Norton's stone "ruin" exhibits some remarkable features, all of which have led Moore to conclude that the structure derives from Celtic or Celtic-related people who migrated from Europe in small numbers and settled in New England some 2,000 years ago, only to later vanish for reasons unknown. The "chamber" itself is an elaborately constructed stone enclosure contained within a large earth-mound. Moore speculates that the structure represents a ritualistic "temple," since it closely corresponds with the small temples present at many European Celtic sites. Deposits of red ochre, a type of ritualistic funerary paint, have been detected within the chamber. Traces of fat-based oil, possibly from ritualistic lamps, also appear in the structure. In front of the chamber's entrance, Moore and his team have unearthed numerous small boulders of white quartz, all of which have been purposefully placed. In Celtic culture, Moore indicates, white quartz had important aesthetic and ritualistic implications associated with Celtic religion. Certainly, he suggests, there is no conceivable reason that a colonial farmer would have so painstakingly positioned these white quartz boulders at the chamber's entrance.

The chamber opens onto a large complex; that is, a roughly 30' x 50' area enclosed by stone walls. Strangely, this entire area in front of the chamber is paved with cobblestone flooring. Again, Moore observes that such a feature has no viable explanation within a colonial context. He believes that this paved area was the site of ritual activity. "The construction here was a labor of love," he says. "This flooring has no utilitarian function. Its implications are aesthetic, and probably ritualistic." Close to the chamber, there is also an elevated terrace, laboriously constructed with massive stones and topped with tremendous slabs of rock. Again, Moore asks, "why would any colonial farmer have bothered to build this?" Moore suggests that the terrace was some type of ritualistic platform. Recently, his team lifted one of the terrace slabs with a hydraulic jack. Excavations beneath the removed slab yielded fragments of worked iron, pottery, and bone, some of which are currently undergoing age-analysis at several laboratories. Moore believes that these artifact fragments may derive from human burials beneath the terrace slabs.

Moore is not alone in this type of research. Dr. Barry Fell, a retired Harvard University professor, has documented many similar "chambers" throughout New England. The best known of these sites is the Mystery Hill complex in Salem, New Hampshire. Here, Fell has studied a vast array of stone chambers, standing henge stones, and stone alters. He claims that numerous inscriptions of "Ogam," an ancient Celtic script, appear at the site, and he concludes that the New Hampshire complex was constructed by Celts who had sailed from Europe during the first millennium B.C. "People deriving from this same culture," Moore suggests, "were likely builders of the chamber in Norton."

Epilogue

Moore's findings are controversial, and some archaeologists would refute them. This writer has had the opportunity to visit the Norton site many times, and even to directly participate in the ongoing excavations there. As I have related to Mr. Moore on numerous occasions, I am firmly of the opinion that I have no opinion! My specialty, after all, pertains to Indian archaeology. I must acknowledge that I do find it difficult to envision some of the chamber's unusual features within a colonial context. However, it will require additional data and findings (C-14 dates, culture-specific artifacts, etc.) before I am comfortably certain that the Norton chamber is derivative of some ancient European culture. Still, I am keeping my mind open to the possibility that Rehoboth's prehistoric Indians may, in fact, have had a few Druid guests!

A MASSACHUSETTS MYSTERY AWAITS RESOLUTION

1675: Southeastern New England erupts—a bloody, frenetic convulsion of inter-cultural mistrust and strife. Indians begin burning farms, English begin burning Indians. Raids, ambushes, decapitations and corpses—atrocities on both sides, with plenty of women and children torn to bloody pieces.

And then, in the summer of 1676, the horror suddenly ceased. The leader of the Wampanoag rebellion (Pometacomet, King Philip) had been killed by English soldiers, as had the Narragansett chief Canochet, the Wampanoags' most crucial military ally.

A renewed calm gradually settled over New England's blood-streaked forest, which just a few months earlier had crackled with musket volley as small groups of Native and English soldiers frenetically took each other apart in various small skirmishes.

The English had prevailed in King Philip's War, but not before they had almost been driven into the sea by enraged Indian raiders and attackers—an ordinarily reasonable Native people who had finally convulsed in rage over colonial mistreatment and land swindle.

The end of King Philip's War marked the virtual end of Native American culture and large-scale Indian political organization in New England. In Massachusetts, the ancient and once-powerful Wampanoag Tribe had been ravaged by the war and by the deprivation of land and resources, so that its people were now dead and disbanded, disillusioned and drunken.

And almost as if symbolic of the tribe's fate, the Wampanoags' only recorded history—in the form of exquisitely beaded wampum belts whose intricately woven symbols and patterns told of their peoples' heritage—suddenly and mysteriously vanished at the end of the war, after they were taken from Philip's subchief and war general, Anawan, when he was captured in Rehoboth by Captain Benjamin Church.

The story of the Wampanoag wampum belts is one that resonates into the present. After more than three centuries since the mysterious disappearance of these visually magnificent and culturally urgent relics (urgent as they contain the only recorded history of the Wampanoag people), there is still an ongoing search for them. In fact, in March of 1995, under the sponsorship of Representative Phil Travis, the Massachusetts House of Representatives passed a Resolution whereby His Excellency John Major, the present Prime Minister of England, was, during a recent visit to that country by Representative Travis, formally queried as to the belts' possible whereabouts (as will be further discussed, records indicate that they might be in England). Additionally, the Resolution called for the return of the belts, if found in Britain, to Massachusetts' small but still extant Wampanoag Nation.

Before further discussion of recent efforts to locate the belts, let us first examine their origin and history:

By the time the belts were captured at Anawan Rock in

Rehoboth by Benjamin Church more than three-hundred years ago, they were already quite old—perhaps centuries so. The belts belonged to the Sachem (tribal chief) of the Wampanoags, and, while they were Philip's belts at the time of the war, they had been passed to him by his father, Chief Massasoit, who had inherited them from his. In other words, like the royal crowns of Europe, the wampum belts passed on a hereditary basis from one Wampanoag ruler to the next. While the royal belts were in his possession, each Sachem was expected to carefully protect them for eventual bequeathment to his royal heir (usually, but not always, his first son), and he was also required by custom to utilize the belts for the recording and transmission of important events in Wampanoag history.

One historian, Milton A. Travers, described the cultural utilization and significance of the belts in this manner, having consulted a knowledgeable Wampanoag source:

> *"In Autumn, the great Sachem of the tribe always ordered one of the most important feasts of the year, called by the Wampanoags 'Nikommosachmiawene.' The council fire was ordered and the warriors and their families would sit about it in a ring composed in the same order and fashion as the War Council. It was during this meeting that the history of the tribe was recounted (which the Sachem read from the beaded wampum belts, whose various woven symbols and scenes depicted important events in the tribe's past), with recent activities appended (by being woven into new bands that were attached to*

169

the existing belts; in this manner, the beaded belts grew longer and longer from one generation to the next, with more and more of the tribes's unfolding history depicted in various woven symbols and pictures).

The oldest male child of each warrior was seated with his father so that he missed nothing of the long history of the tribe as read by the chief from his royal wampum belt. It was the custom to have the history of the tribe depicted on the broad bands of the belts, and the belts themselves, when not being used in this manner for teaching tribal history, were actually worn by the royal Sachem. The belts were passed around the group from one to another and read aloud, each holder interpreting the events depicted thereon. The belts depicted in designs of wampum (beads wrought from clam shell) the great victories, and the mighty warriors who gained glory on the warpath before them. They also told of the defeats and loss of territory to rival tribes. They told of the days of famine, sickness and plague...in short, these belts were the only historical documents the Wampanoags had of their lives and those of their ancestors before them. This was their precious heritage for the descendants to keep and pass on to posterity. It was the sacred duty of the great Sachem to guard and preserve these royalties."

More specifically, what did the royal Wampanoag wampum

belts actually look like? As described in colonial writings after the belts were taken from Anawan (who, during the war, had been protecting them for the militarily preoccupied Philip), the belts were *"...nine inches broad in black and white figures and flowers, and many pictures of birds and beasts...(the belts), when hung upon Captain Church, reached his ankles. Another belt of wampum...had two flags on the back part which hung down his back, and another small belt with a star upon the end of it."*

And what of the belts' mysterious fate? In his writings about the war, Captain Church indicates that Anawan willingly volunteered the belts to the English at the time of his surrender in Rehoboth. However, considering their sacred and central cultural importance to the Wampanoags, it seems difficult to imagine that Anawan would treat these artifacts so lightly (such a scenario would be comparable to the ancient Israelites gleefully volunteering to hand over the Arc of the Covenant— their most crucially central and sacred cultural artifact—to some enemy or another. So sacred were the wampum belts, in fact, that they can be accurately deemed the "Torah", of sorts, of the Wampanoag people). To this writer, anyway, it seems more likely that these sacred items were forcibly taken, a premise which would be consistent with Anawan's treatment subsequent to his capture (after promises of fair treatment from Captain Church, the aged Anawan was marched to Plymouth and promptly put to death by order of the General Court).

Whether or not acquired by force, the belts, once captured by Church, were eventually passed on to Governor Winslow of Plymouth Colony, who supposedly sent them overseas to the

English King as tribute and as verification that the Indian "problem" in the King's subject New England colony had been settled once and for all with the fall of Philip.

It is uncertain if the belts ever reached their destination. Governor Winslow had entrusted the belts to his brother-in-law, Waldergrave Pelham, with instructions that they be transported to the King at Whitehall in England. Several years later, however, after being told about the belts, the King of England wrote Winslow to state that he had never received them. Of course, trans-Atlantic sea travel of the 1600's was slow and unreliable, so it remains somewhat possible that the King finally did receive the belts at some later date. The records of Plymouth Colony, as well as those of the King's court at Whitehall in England, are simply not clear on the matter.

In this writer's opinion, there are four possible answers to the mystery of the belts' ultimate fate:

1) Winslow's brother-in-law, Waldergrave Pelham, after being entrusted with transport of the belts to the king may have chosen instead to break them apart for their valuable wampum shell beads. (Interestingly, Pelham was in debt at the time, and Native wampum beads were circulating currency in early colonial New England.) Pelham, perhaps thinking that he could convincingly blame the belts' disappearance on the unreliable shipping of the time, may have pillaged them for their valuable wampum, though such a theory remains entirely speculative.

2) The belts were possibly placed on a boat bound for England,

but may have been lost due to careless handling. As it is unknown what boat was used for the transport, it is also possible that the ship was pirated and/or sunk before reaching Britain—a not-infrequent occurrence in those early days of precarious trans-Atlantic travel.

3) The belts possibly did reach the King but, with no understanding of their cultural significance, His Majesty perhaps deemed them to be trivial items. In this case, the belts may have been quickly discarded, perhaps even given to one of the royal children as a plaything. Subsequently, the belts were perhaps quickly lost or destroyed.

4) The belts possibly did reach England, may have been placed in some depository, and perhaps remain in England, obscurely hidden in the basement of one museum or another, to the present day.

It is this last potential scenario, which is perhaps as likely as any other, that has fueled attempts by certain local individuals to discover the whereabouts of the belts in England and to hopefully bring them home to Massachusetts, given their great cultural significance to New England.

More recently, the issue of the belts' whereabouts was raised several years ago by the late Dr. Maurice Robbins, former state archaeologist for Massachusetts. Before his death in 1990, Dr. Robbins discussed the issue with Rehoboth resident Robert T. Sharples, then Chairman of the Rehoboth Historical Commission. Later that year, Mr. Sharples composed and forwarded a letter to England's Prince Charles, requesting information about the belts' prospective existence in England and their possible return to the United States. Charles never responded.

Sharples was persistent in his efforts, however, and he eventually discussed the issue with Representative Phil Travis. Subsequently, Travis was instrumental in securing passage of the above-mentioned Resolution from the Massachusetts House of Representatives, calling upon England to locate the belts and to return them to this state.

During a recent visit to England, Travis deposited the Resolution with the appropriate British officials. He also made inquiries at various British museums and artifactual depositories in an unsuccessful attempt to locate the belts. On March 15, 1995, Travis received a letter from 10 Downing Street, from an official at the Prime Minister's office, which reads in part as follows:

> *"The Prime Minister understands the concern of the Massachusetts Legislature to find out what happened to the 'Wampum Belts.' Given the uncertainty over what became of them in 1676, and the length of time which has passed since then, the prospects of finding evidence about the belts are not good. But the Prime Minister has asked the Department of National Heritage to do everything it can to look into this matter. We will let you know the result of their investigations."*

Travis' efforts have apparently resulted in what might become

174

the most thorough and comprehensive search to date in England. Assuming the British promise of "investigations" is a valid one (this writer has reviewed the letter from John Major's office; the Prime Minister's office seems quite sincere in its promise to initiate a search through England's Department of National Heritage), then the belts just might, at some point in the near future, make a surprise reappearance after three centuries of obscurity. This would be an extraordinary historical development for Massachusetts, for New England, and, especially, for modern-day Wampanoags, whose partially lost history is depicted on the belts and who, if the artifacts are found, should ultimately take possession of them.

More likely, however, and sadly, the belts will probably never reappear. More than 300 years have elapsed since any written reference to their whereabouts, and there is no certainty that they ever reached the shores of Britain. Relics of a turbulent and disturbed period in New England history, the belts, like many Native American customs and traditions, are likely the casualty of cultural indifference.